The Band Director's Brain Bank

by

R. Jack Mercer, M.M.E.

Chairman of Music Department and

Director of Bands

Chaffey High School, Ontario, California

Library of Congress Catalog Card No. 75-132449

The Instrumentalist Co.
1418 Lake Street
Evanston, Illinois 60204

R. Jack Mercer is currently director of bands at Chaffey High School in Ontario, California. He holds the Bachelor of Music and Master of Music degrees from Northwestern University. Prior to coming to California, he taught instrumental music in the public schools of Michigan, at Lincoln College in Lincoln, Illinois, and at the University of Iowa Laboratory School. In 1966 his marching band at Chaffey High School and its drill team combined with the school choir and flag corps to present the halftime show at the All Star Pro-Bowl football game held in the Los Angeles Coliseum. Entitled "The Cost of Freedom," the show earned the Freedom Foundation Award of Valley Forge as a contributing force toward patriotism in the United States. Mercer is a member of the Board of Advisors for The Instrumentalist magazine.

CONTENTS

Introduction

Although my education and experience have given me an intimate acquaintance with music education in American public schools, my training in public school music did not equip me with all the skills necessary to write this book. Nowhere in my background did I learn the intricacies of developing a questionnaire, the rules for selecting a valid sample, the skills of data processing and statistical analysis, and the painful process of interpreting the meaning of empirical data.

After spending four-and-a-half months interviewing band directors, I found it most intriguing to proceed to record their responses on IBM cards and decipher the critical issues raised by their responses.

For assistance in all these matters, I wish to thank my wife, Jane, who is Associate Professor in Sociology at the University of California, Riverside. From the beginning she acted as advisor, consultant, and interpreter. She supervised the developing of the questionnaire, the method of selecting the sample, and suggested the interview techniques used in collecting the data.

I am deeply indebted to the 222 band directors who took time from their busy schedules to talk with me. Their kindness and hospitality were deeply appreciated during my long, lonely trip around the United States.

I also wish to thank the following people for reading and editing the manuscript: Ulla E. Bauers, Kleo D. Martin, Allan G. Smith, Glenn L. Fisher, June and Dick Lewis, and the members of my family, Ronald, Robert and Ann.

For 25 years I have worked as a band director in Michigan, Iowa, and California. These experiences have made me aware of broad differences in music education in different regions of the United States. In Michigan, most directors encourage their bandsmen to develop performing ability through completing a series of proficiency examinations. In Iowa, most directors use a "conservatory" approach to teaching music which emphasizes private lessons and intensive work in small groups. In California, the flood of families migrating to the state has made individual lessons almost impossible and the emphasis is on section rehearsals.

It was this variation which prompted me to wonder about the teaching methods being used by directors in other regions. Locked in by geography and the day-to-day responsibility of conducting a band program, I had only the most cursory knowledge of the techniques used by other directors throughout the nation. This interest gradually evolved into a concrete plan and the research reported in this book.

At the outset, my goal was conceptualized as a *Band Director's Brain Bank* which would report, systematically, on the methods and techniques being used by the most successful band directors. I hoped to secure information and insight into common problems such as scheduling, student drop-outs, finances, lesson programs, student evaluation, and so forth. Thus my interview schedule asked detailed questions about budget, programming, rehearsals, and band organization. I planned to share this information with others who might also be interested in learning fresh ways to conduct their instrumental departments.

However, as I began to study and to process the interviews, an unexpected picture of instrumental music education emerged. I began to see the critical issues and dilemmas in public school education for the first time and changed my original plan for this volume. In addition to a "brain bank" it has become a mirror reflecting a panoramic view of instrumental music in the United States.

Chapter I

The Research Plan

The brisk October air is charged with excitement as the first half ends. Tired gladiators of the gridiron jog from the field as the crisp staccato of 20 field drums punctuates the air.

At the sound of some 200 instruments heralding the halftime show, spectators, who were moving from their seats toward the refreshment stands, hesitate and sit down again. The fanfare! Four-hundred band and drill team members march onto an empty field which seems to shrink when they fill it.

As they step down the field, intricate geometric designs unfold, accentuated by the flash of orange and yellow pom-poms. Colorful formations are interspersed with precision drills and dance routines. The versatile performance produces a roar of appreciation from the 98,000 spectators.

We are witnessing a segment of public school music not found elsewhere in the world. This is a scene duplicated in this country a thousand times over each fall weekend. Stadiums may vary from a monstrous coliseum to a field lined by portable bleachers. Crowds may vary from a few hundred to a hundred thousand. But the thrill, the color, the music, and the pageantry remain.

Indeed, instrumental music holds such an accepted place in the public schools that few question its presence or ask for a justification of its existence beyond the drama of the gridiron and the inspiration of the concert stage.

However, in recent years, there has been a growing emphasis on scientific and academic achievement. The mood of the nation is shifting. The arts and humanities are being asked to justify their place in the curriculum. Placed on the defensive, music educators are forced to ask themselves:

"How can we justify the time and money spent on the instrumental music program in the public schools? Are there changes which we should be making? If so, what are they?"

The customary clichés no longer satisfy our critics nor ourselves. But where can we find a comprehensive picture of instrumental music in America today? Where are the data on which to base a thorough evaluation? Where can we find answers to these seemingly simple questions: How much do high schools, on the average, spend each year on their instrumental programs? Why are some bands and orchestras rated outstanding while others are not? What are the qualities of directors who are rated outstanding by their colleagues? What percentage of the students in a typical high school actually participate in instrumental music?

In pondering these questions I concluded that music education needed a systematic, carefully designed study which could furnish broad answers to these questions and provide the information necessary for a comprehensive assessment. Consequently, I decided to seek answers to some basic questions by doing a nationwide study of high school band programs, not by mailing questionnaires but by interviewing each band director individually.

While persons in other disciplines have made numerous studies of their fields using scientifically designed research procedures, the field of music education has been slow in following their lead. To my knowledge, there are no national studies of music education based on survey research methods. There are no investigations which compare large and small high schools, or examine the financial and community support which bands receive. No information is available which analyzes the personality of the director as a factor in the development of an outstanding music department. Nor has there been any attempt to determine whether problems facing music teachers in one region of our nation differ from problems being faced in other regions. As music educators, we need insights based on empirical studies. We need to pool the best thoughts and experience of our profession and to think through the direction music education will take. It is this research vacuum which prompted my 17,567 mile trip to interview directors widely scattered throughout the continental United States.

Selecting States and Schools to Visit

It was obvious from the beginning that I would not have the time, energy, nor the financial resources to visit every state during the spring semester for which I had a sabbatical leave. However, I did want to include at least one state from each of the major geographic regions of the country — the Pacific Northwest, the Pacific Southwest, the Southwest, the Southeast, the Northeast, and the Midwest. Limited by a four-and-a-half month travel schedule, it was necessary to select a combination of states which would form a logical travel route and which could be covered in a spring semester. The final itinerary included Texas, Florida, New York, Michigan, Illinois, Indiana, Iowa, Missouri, Kansas, Colorado, Washington, Oregon, and my home state of California. Figure 1 is a map of my route.

Figure 1-1

Map Of The Travel Route

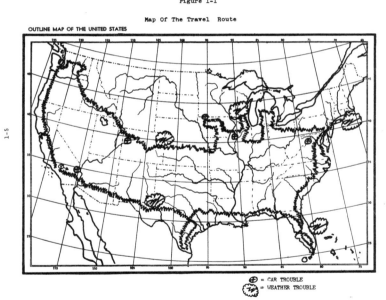

OUTLINE MAP OF THE UNITED STATES

⊕ = CAR TROUBLE
= WEATHER TROUBLE

It would have been better if I could have included more states from New England as well as more states in the South. However, there wasn't time to travel the great distances which would have been required to cover each of these sections thoroughly.

Weather was also a factor. A late winter blizzard drastically limited my travel in the New England states, so that I was not even able to complete the interviews I had planned. More complete coverage of these regions must be left for another time and another study.

In addition to regional coverage, I wanted the study to include both large and small high schools. Having spent 10 years in a high school with 400 students in rural Iowa, I have always been interested in the problems of the band director in small high schools. Scheduling, recruiting, and budgeting problems are considerably different in a school of 400 than they are in a school of 4,000. How could both large and small high schools be included in the sample so that they could be compared?

Originally, I intended to interview only the outstanding large and small high school bands in each state. However, as I began to work out the research design, it became clear that I could not understand the unique characteristics of outstanding bands unless I had a comparison group consisting of bands with less notable programs. For example, we frequently hear directors say that they believe the success of a music department is related to the amount of money the director has to spend. To test this hypothesis, it is necessary to compare the budgets of outstanding music departments with those of less outstanding departments to see if there are any significant differences. Without a control group, it is not possible to determine whether outstanding departments have significantly more money to spend than other departments.

Therefore, the central problems in the research design were to identify the outstanding bands in each state, to select a control group of less outstanding bands, and to assure that both large and small high schools would appear in the sample.

Those persons most likely to be in a position to offer consistent, reliable information about the quality of various instrumental music departments in their state are the university and college band directors. They are usually involved in judging music contests and frequently travel throughout the state to hear performances. More than any other group of musicians, they are likely to have an overview of the entire state. Therefore, I asked the university and college band directors to nominate the outstanding departments in their state for inclusion in this study.

The system had to be simple as well as comprehensive. I did not want to use an open-ended question which would simply ask directors to recall from memory the best groups they had heard. With such an unstructured question, they could overlook a school in some section of the state they had not visited recently, or forget a small department with an excellent program. So I decided to develop two comprehensive lists of the high schools in each of the states to be visited. One list would include all the high schools with a student population of between 400 and 999 students and the other would contain the names of all high schools having a thousand or more students.

The California Department of Education publishes a comprehensive directory of all public and private schools in the state by size. I surmised that similar lists would be available through the education departments of other states. Therefore, I sent a letter to the Department of Education in the capital city of each of the states I planned to visit, requesting a copy of the state directory of public schools.

The first directory arrived from New York, the most distant state on the itinerary. One morning the mail contained a very large package from Albany, weighing several pounds and costing three dollars in prepaid postage. Puzzled by its size, I opened the package to find a complete IBM print-out of all the schools in New York State. Since there was no directory available, officials had been kind enough to lend me one of the state computer listings which I later returned.

Other directories were not quite so formidable nor so prompt in arriving. Directories were out of print in three states and it was necessary to ask the college judges to make their nominations without the benefit of a master list to aid them in their selections.

As the directories were received, a list of the large and small high schools in each state was typed in the form of ballots, leaving a space before the name of each high school for the college director to place his evaluation. The instructions asked the college director to select the ten schools on the small school ballot which had the most outstanding departments and to rank them from one to ten. He was asked to repeat the same rating procedure for the large high schools. (A copy of the letter sent to college directors is reproduced in Appendix A.)

As the ballots were returned to me, the rank orders assigned by the college directors' nominations were used to determine the outstanding schools. Each director's first choice was awarded ten points. His second choice was given nine points, his third choice received eight points, and so forth. When a school was nominated by more than one college director, points were added together for a total score. The returns from the balloting for the large high schools in Texas are shown in Table 1.

The first ranked school in the large school classification was nominated by nine judges who gave the department a total of 57 nomination points. There was a tie for third place — two schools each received a total of 43 points. However, one school was mentioned by eight judges, while the other was mentioned by only six judges. Therefore, the school mentioned by eight judges was given the higher rating. The first five schools on each list were given interview priority. However, in cases in which the director was unavailable, or the travel route impossible, lower ranked schools were selected to serve as alternates, beginning with the school ranked sixth. Thus, five outstanding large bands were visited in each state.

Table 1

Results of Texas Balloting by College and University
Directors for *Large* High Schools

Name of High School	Points Received from Each of Nine Judges									Total number of judges nominating the school	Total Points
	1	2	3	4[a]	5	6	7	8	9		
First ranked school [b]	9	10	9	5	4	5	5	5	5	9	57
Second ranked school [b]	5	0	0	5	7	10	9	9	10	7	55
Third ranked school [b]	4	4	4	5	6	0	5	7	8	8	43
Fourth ranked school [b]	6	9	0	5	10	0	10	3	0	6	43
Fifth ranked school [b]	3	7	0	5	0	0	9	0	4	4	28
Alternates											
Sixth ranked school [b]	0	8	8	5	0	0	0	0	0	3	21
Seventh ranked school [b]	0	0	0	5	0	4	5	6	0	4	20
Eighth ranked school	0	1	7	5	0	3	0	0	0	4	16
Ninth ranked school	0	5	10	0	0	0	0	0	0	2	15
Tenth ranked school	0	6	0	0	0	8	0	0	0	2	14

[a] When the university judges used check marks rather than ranking the schools from one to ten, all checked
schools received five nominating points.

[b] Directors actually interviewed and included in sample.

Selecting the outstanding bands among the small high schools of
each state proved more difficult, because they were not as well-known
to the college and university directors as the large schools. Table 2
shows the result of the balloting in Texas.

Table 2

Results of Texas Balloting by College and University
Directors for *Small* High Schools

Name of High School	Points Received from Each of Nine Judges									Total Number of judges nominating the school	Total Points
	1	2	3	4[a]	5	6	7	8	9		
First ranked school [b]	10	0	5	0	9	0	8	0	0	4	32
Second ranked school [b]	6	6	0	5	5	3	0	0	4	6	29
Third ranked school [b]	0	0	4	5	0	8	6	5	0	5	28
Fourth ranked school [b]	2	10	0	0	0	0	10	0	0	3	22
Fifth ranked school [b]	3	0	0	0	5	6	0	5	0	4	19
Alternates											
Sixth ranked school	0	9	0	0	0	3	0	5	0	3	17
Seventh ranked school	9	0	6	0	0	0	0	0	0	2	15
Eighth ranked school	0	0	2	0	0	7	3	0	0	3	12
Ninth ranked school	0	0	0	5	0	0	4	0	1	3	10
Tenth ranked school	0	0	9	0	0	0	0	0	0	1	9

[a] When the university judges used check marks rather than ranking the schools from one to ten, all checked
schools received five nominating points.

[b] Directors actually interviewed and included in sample.

I later visited several of the college directors who had submitted nominations. When I questioned them about the scarcity of small school nominations on their ballots, they replied that it was difficult to keep track of the small schools because of the constant turnover in directors. A small school might have its music department department blossom briefly under an enterprising, enthusiastic director, only to decline when he moved to another school district. They reported that there is less fluctuation in the quality of the program in larger schools which have larger staffs.

The number of college directors serving as nominators varied from state to state, since some states have many more colleges and universities than others. The response to my letter requesting nominations also varied from state to state. The scores from Texas are based on the votes of nine judges; the scores from Florida are based on six judges; New York, seven judges; Michigan, four judges; Indiana, seven judges; Illinois, six judges; Iowa, five judges; Missouri, seven judges; Kansas, two judges; Colorado, two judges; Washington State, five judges; Oregon, three judges; and California, nine judges.

As the ballots were returned, all nominated schools were plotted on a map. Although there was some interesting geographic clustering, the nominated schools were frequently widely scattered throughout the state, and it was sometimes necessary to substitute a school with fewer nomination points for those located in an isolated part of the state.

After determining the nominated schools for each state, the next problem was to select a non-nominated school which would match each nominated school in size and geographic location. Using my comprehensive list of the high schools in each state, I located the closest non-nominated high school with a student body of approximately the same size as that of the nominated school. Seventy-nine per cent of the matching large schools were within 50 miles of their nominated twin. There were isolated difficulties in finding close geographical matches for a few large nominated schools. For example, Key West, Florida, had to be matched with a school more than 200 miles away. However, 93% of the matching small schools were within 50 miles of their counterparts. Table 3 gives a complete picture of all the schools taking part in the study.

Although the original research design called for interviews with five nominated large school directors and five nominated small school directors in each state, completed interviews varied somewhat from this pattern. Only in Indiana did I actually get five interviews with each type of school.

It was possible to complete twice as many interviews with nominated large schools (70) as with nominated small schools (35). In my home state of California, I was able to complete three times as many

7

Table 3
COMPLETED INTERVIEWS BY STATE AND CATEGORY OF SCHOOL

STATE	Bands nominated by college directors "Nominated Bands"			Band matched to nominated schools by location and size "Matched Bands"				
	LARGE SCHOOLS 1,000 + STUDENTS	SMALL SCHOOLS 400-999 STUDENTS	TOTAL NOMINATED SCHOOLS	LARGE SCHOOLS 1,000 + STUDENTS	SMALL SCHOOLS 400-999 STUDENTS	TOTAL MATCHED SCHOOLS	TOTAL MISCEL. SCHOOLS	TOTAL INTERVIEWED
TEXAS	7	4	11	7	4	11	6	28
FLORIDA	6	4	10	6	4	10	0	20
NEW YORK	4	1	5	4	1	5	0	10
MICHIGAN	5	5	10	5	5	10	0	20
INDIANA	7	3	10	7	2	9	1	20
ILLINOIS	5	2	7	4	2	6	5	18
IOWA	4	4	8	4	4	8	3	19
MISSOURI	2	2	4	2	2	4	0	8
KANSAS	1	1	2	0	0	0	4	6
COLORADO	4	1	5	2	0	2	0	7
WASHINGTON	5	3	8	4	2	6	0	14
OREGON	4	3	7	2	1	3	0	10
CALIFORNIA	16	2	18	16	2	18	6	42
TOTALS	70	35	105	63	29	92	25	222

interviews with nominated large schools as originally intended. However, in some states, such as Missouri and Kansas, where schools were widely scattered geographically, time did not permit as many interviews. These variations in coverage must be taken into account when evaluating the findings.

There were 63 interviews completed out of the 70 matched pairs for the large schools and 29 completed interviews out of the 35 matched pairs among small high schools. Altogether, interviews were completed at 105 nominated schools (70 large and 35 small), and 92 matched schools (63 large and 29 small). This was a total of 197 interviews which conformed to the original plan calling for matched pairs of nominated and non-nominated schools.

A critical consideration in research is the efficiency of the matching of the pairs finally interviewed. Small nominated schools had an average of 691 in their student bodies as compared to 707 in the small matched schools, an average difference of only 16 students. The average size of the large nominated schools was 2061 students, while the average size of the matched large schools was 1926. This is an average difference of 135 students. Neither difference, however, is statistically significant.

Circumstances occasionally made it possible to interview directors who were neither in the nominated nor in the matched sample. Information from these 25 non-sample interviews is not included in the statistical comparisons which are included in the Appendix. However, when information gained in the non-sample interviews is relevant, it is used and indicated in the text. Most of the extra interviews were held in Texas, Illinois, Iowa, Kansas, and California. Altogether, I completed 222 interviews during my four and a half months in the field.

Preparing for the Field Work

It took several months to write and rewrite questions for the interview schedule. When the questionnaire finally seemed complete, I sent it to several music educators, asking them to indicate questions that were not clear and to point out areas which might have been overlooked. The interview schedule was greatly improved as a result of their suggestions.

Remaining difficulties were eliminated after a series of pretest interviews with several California directors who were willing to offer suggestions. Thus, with the assistance of many colleagues, I formulated the final questionnaire.

The interview was divided into three parts. The first consisted of structured questions about the band program, the school district, and the director's personal and educational background. Most of the questions in this section were precoded, that is, the response categories were worked out in advance so that the answers could be circled by the interviewer at the time the question was asked.

After completing the structured questions, each director was asked to complete the second part, a "semantic differential" scale on himself and his students (Osgood, 1969). [1] A more detailed explanation of these scales appears in chapter nine.

The third portion of the interview was a questionnaire which the director completed himself. He placed a check mark next to the response category that came closest to describing his own opinion on various issues. These questions focused mainly on the director's educational philosophy and his attitudes toward other faculty members, students, and the community.

The fall football season came and went. Between halftime performances and my other obligations, I counted ballots, identified nominated schools, selected matching schools, and pretested the interview schedule. On February 1, I typed the final stencil of the 24-page questionnaire and mimeographed 400 copies.

The problem of putting all 9600 pages together was solved by laying the 24 stacks of pages on several long tables in the hall just inside the band building. As the 200 bandsmen arrived for rehearsal, each was asked to assemble two sets of 24 sheets. When every bandsman had gone through the assembly line twice, the 400 questionnaires were assembled. It took less than 30 minutes. Then four husky boys made two trips to carry them out to my trailer. By noon I was ready to start the journey and the interviewing.

The Field Work

My sabbatical leave covered a span of two years rather than one. The first half was approved for the spring semester which was spent traveling and completing the 222 interviews. After returning to teach six weeks in summer school and to direct the marching band in the fall semester, I spent the second half of my sabbatical, the next spring semester, analyzing the information collected and writing the first draft of my findings.

Texas was the first state on the itinerary. As I drove across the deserts of the Southwest, I decided to approach each director by making a person-to-person long distance call about two days in advance of my intended arrival. School switchboard operators and principals give high priority to an out-of-town call and often interrupt a class, send messages, or, if necessary, form a search party in order to notify their band director that he has a long distance call.

By asking the operator to secure the first and last name of the director before putting him on the line, I had all of the preliminary information needed to set up an appointment for the interview. When the director picked up his telephone, I knew his name and the name of the school in which he worked. Once connected, I had three minutes to arouse his interest in my study and convince him that he should invest two hours of his time in an interview.

Imagine that you have just arrived at school. Your telephone rings and the long distance operator connects you with a voice that says, "Hello, my name is Jack Mercer. I'm a band director from Chaffey High School in Ontario, California. Would you believe that I am traveling 17,600 miles just to visit with you?" This approach immediately aroused both curiosity and some reservations. It takes some readjusting of schedules for a director to find a two-hour block of time in which to be interviewed during the day. Some directors were kind enough to come to school an hour early; others scheduled the interview for the period just before noon and then continued responding to questions during lunch. Frequently, the last period of the day was extended into the after school hours so as to allow enough time for completing the interview. Several directors rearranged their entire schedule for the day to make the interview possible. Others were able to find substitutes to teach their classes for them while they were being interviewed.

I found that directors were generally cautious during the first few minutes of each interview. Many suspected I was trying to sell them something and were waiting for the sales pitch. When none came, the relationship usually became more friendly and some directors invited me to their homes for the evening and, occasionally, even invited me for supper. This allowed ample time to extend our conversation.

There were times, however, when a director could only visit with me for about an hour and some questions had to be omitted. As a result, in later chapters some statistical tables show fewer responses than the total 197 directors.

Several times during the trip a director's schedule was so full and complicated that it was impossible for him to arrange time for an interview and he had to be eliminated from the sample. My only outright refusal, however, came from one of the two women band directors who appeared in the sample. I later learned from another director in her state that she was having discipline problems and the board of education was considering dismissing her. It is conceivable that she thought that I was an investigator hired by the school district. At any rate, she refused to see me.

Analyzing the Data

My interviewing schedule provided 65,000 individual responses to 340 questions in each interview. These were translated into coded numbers which represented particular answers and these numbers were keypunched on IBM cards. The responses for each director filled nine IBM cards. Once the information was punched on data cards, it was then tabulated by a computer programmed to compare nominated with matched schools, large schools with small schools, schools in different regions with each other, and so forth.

Three major statistical tests were used to determine whether differences between the nominated and matched schools were large enough that they probably did not occur by chance. The t test is used when the information being compared is numerical, such as age, size of school, or number of students in the band. It compares the averages of two groups to see if one average is significantly higher or lower than the other. A significant difference is one which would not occur more than five times in a hundred by chance. In general, a t of 2.0 or higher meets this qualification. This is written p .05. A t of 2.6 happens less than one time in a hundred by chance. This means that the difference between the two groups being compared is even more significant than a t of 2.0. This would be written p .01. Some t's are so large they would happen only one time in a thousand by chance. This is true of any t of 3.4 or higher, and is written p .001.

The chi square test was also used to test for statistical differences. This test is used when the information being compared is not numerical but is categorical or nominal, i.e. comparisons of religion, sex, or race. It compares the number of persons in a particular category in one group with the number of persons in the same category in another group to see if the difference in the proportion of the two groups in each category is large enough so that it is not likely to have happened by chance.

A third statistical procedure is correlational analysis. This technique determines the extent to which two characteristics change together. For this type of analysis, simple linear correlations between two variables (Pearson's r) are used.

When findings are discussed in later chapters, I will not complicate the text by reporting every t, X^2, or r. The analysis does not consider any difference between two groups worthy of consideration if the probabilities are more than five in a hundred that the difference could be due to chance.

Acknowledgments

I am grateful to the following people who were generous enough to take time to read my interview schedule and to indicate those questions that were not clear as well as to suggest additional ideas: Justin Burston, Keynote Music Service, Inc.; Robert Greenwell, Supervisor of Music, Baldwin Park, California; Truman Hutton, Supervisor of Music, Los Angeles City Schools; Fred Ohlendorf, Supervisor of Music, Long Beach, California; Robert Reynolds, Director of Bands, California State College, Long Beach (now Director of Bands at the University of Wisconsin, Madison); Traugott Rohner, Publisher of *The Instrumentalist* magazine; and Clarence Sawhill, Director of Bands, University of California, Los Angeles.

I would like to thank the following directors for helping me finalize the interview schedule: Ben Baker, Montclair High School, Montclair, California; Dean Bruington, Chino High School, Chino, California; Mervin Corner, Alta Loma High School, Alta Loma, California; Robin Snyder, La Verne High School, La Verne, California; Richard Wagnon, Santa Monica High School, Santa Monica, California; and Elbert Warren, Upland High School, Upland, California.

Chapter II

Performance,
Its History and Its Pressures

As the findings of this study began to emerge, it became apparent that many of the traditions which are a part of our educational philosophy today are anchored in the past. An example of this is the emphasis placed on performance in American public schools.

On entering the band room of 222 schools I was constantly aware of trophies, plaques, and medals covering the walls of the rehearsal hall. Blue ribbons, letters of commendation, and certificates of merit filled the bulletin boards reflecting the active performance schedules of the high school bands.

During the interview each band director described his performance schedule for the previous year. The band in the typical high school with an enrollment of over 1,000 students gives an average of 6.6 halftime shows and 5.5 concerts per year. It also participates in 3.3 parades. This is an average of 15.4 large group performances in a typical school year.

Small high school bands are almost as active. The band in the average small high school presents 6.0 halftime shows and 4.7 concerts per year and participates in 3.8 parades. This is an average of 14.5 performances in a school year. *In other words, the typical high school band gives an average of 1.5 performances a month during the school year — a large group performance every two-and-a half weeks!*

There are many school bands which are extremely active. One Southern high school reported giving 16 halftime shows, another gave 15, and a third 14. The average number of halftime performances in the southern region is 10.3 — twice as high as the number reported by other regions. Southern band directors still participate in an average of three parades and give an average of five concerts a year. They present an average of 18.2 major performances a year — one every two weeks. Bands in the Great Lakes region rank second with an average of 14.3 performances per school year, Pacific Coast bands rank third with 13.7, and Midwest bands (other than Great Lakes) are lowest with 12.2.

Why is there so much emphasis in American public school music on training the performing musican and relatively little on training the listener? The situation is almost completely reversed in many European schools.

In some countries, music is compulsory for all students through the tenth grade but training is primarily in music appreciation, with special emphasis on the works of national composers. Public school music in Europe emphasizes training the listener and gives little attention to training the performer while public school music in America emphasizes training the performer and gives less attention to training the listener. The reason for this antithesis in music education can be traced historically.

Organized Instrumental Music

Organized instrumental music first made its appearance in America at the turn of the 19th century when Gottlieb Graupner, a German immigrant, arrived in America and immediately set himself to the task of building an orchestra in Boston. His mastery of the oboe, piano, clarinet, and string bass equipped him with sufficient musical knowledge to attract capable musicians to his organization. By 1882, his orchestra was giving regular public performances.

These pioneering efforts by Gottlieb Graupner earned him the title of "Father of the American Orchestra" and eventually led to the organization of the Boston Symphony Orchestra. Following the plan of many foreign orchestras (mostly amateur or semi-professional) which precede each concert by an open public rehearsal (for which admission is charged) the Boston Symphony Orchestra successfully launched its first annual series of 20 concerts on October 22, 1881. In 1889, the city fathers voted to build a symphony hall, thus giving the Boston Symphony a permanent place in Boston society.

Another early American orchestra was also the work of German musicians. Following the Revolution of 1848, 23 German refugees fled to America. Finding themselves alone and without friends, they decided to organize an orchestra. Carl Zerrahn, first flutist in this "Germania Orchestra," led the group in concerts in Boston, Philadelphia, and New York.

In 1854, Zerrahn assumed leadership of the Handel and Haydn Society and, in 1865, also accepted responsibility for conducting the Harvard Symphony Concerts.

The Moravians in America likewise were among the first groups to organize musical societies, both vocal and instrumental. They brought their Bohemia-Germanic love for music with them and gave some of the earliest American performances of the music of Haydn and Mozart. Their unique trombone choir continues to this day and some of their own composers wrote charming music, which was considerably more sophisticated that that being written by native American composers of that period.

Although bands made an early appearance, they did not attract much public support. As early as 1773, J. Flagg established a band in Boston but there is no record of how long it survived. After the Revolutionary War, military bands began to evolve. At that time, the West Point Band, considered the best in the country, consisted of two flutes, five clarinets, one bassoon, one trumpet, one bugle, two horns, one trombone, and one drum (Elson, 1904, p. 42).

However, it wasn't until 1853 that bands really first excited American audiences. It was a whirlwind promoter and showman from France who ignited the nation's interest in bands. Antoine Jullien, the son of a French bandmaster, was giving financially unsuccessful band concerts in France and England when he heard that Americans, hungry for music and entertainment, were receiving European artists with enthusiasm and monetary rewards. He learned that musicians from England, France, Italy, and Germany had fled to America following the revolutions in Europe in the 1840's. Convinced that his future lay in America, he sailed to New York, auditioned the best refugee musicians he could find, and organized the first professional band ever seen in the United States.

Using bombastic promotional tactics, he broadcast his presence with huge posters, handbills, and flamboyant invitations to the most important persons in the music world. To entice his audiences to his concerts, he displayed "the world's largest ophicleide" (an early type of keyed tuba), as well as " the world's largest bass drum." His audiences discovered that everything promised in the front page stories which appeared in every New York newspaper actually occurred at each concert.

Among those sitting in the 1854 Boston audience watching Jullien's extravaganzas was a 23-year-old who had assumed the directorship of the Boston Brass Band only two years earlier, Patrick Gilmore. Young and impressionable, he accepted Jullien's grandiose methods and for 40 years, incorporated them into his own musical career.

Gilmore, a talented cornetist, proved to be an even greater showman than Jullien. He developed his modest regimental band into a world-renowned concert band which toured both Europe and America.

His flare for the spectacular originated the National Peace Jubilee following the Civil War. Intended to be a message of peace and joy which would be carried into every corner of the nation, the celebration included plans for a coliseum to seat an audience of 50,000, an adult chorus of 10,000, an orchestra of 1,000, a children's chorus of 20,000, as well as the largest pipe organ in America.

The program opened on the afternoon of June 15, 1869 with the coliseum filled to capacity and the doors shut to keep back the hundreds of people pressing from the outside for admittance. The Jubilee gave its listeners excitement in sound never before heard by an American audience and for five days they responded with frenzied applause.

Thus, Patrick Gilmore, a poor immigrant boy from Athlone, Ireland, became the "Father of American Bands."

In the 1870's, hundreds of small town bands were being organized all over the nation. By 1875, when Gilmore began his cross-country tours, he was welcomed and enthusiastically supported by the many local bands. For nearly 20 years, Gilmore traveled to hundreds of communities. Although he did not consider himself a music educator, his band furnished a pattern for many hometown organizations. He pioneered new directions in band sound, instrumentation, and showmanship which were widely imitated by his professional colleagues

At one of the celebrated fairs of the day, there was a young musician playing first violin in Offenbach's orchestra, which was appearing on an alternating schedule with the Gilmore Band. His name was John Philip Sousa. Only 21 years old, the young Sousa spent his free hours listening intently to the Gilmore Band. In 1880, when Sousa became conductor of the United States Marine Corps Band, he began drawing on this experience. Like Gilmore, Sousa organized his own professional band in 1892 and began to cross and recross the continent playing in every state in the nation and in Canada. Between 1900 and 1905 he made four European tours. Between 1892 and 1932 he spent 28 million dollars on salaries and transportation. His success can be measured both in his musical achievements and in the inspiration he furnished to community and school bands all over the nation.

Bombarded by men such as Jullien, Gilmore, and Sousa, America became band conscious. In the years prior to the radio, the phonograph, the movies, and the horseless carriage, bands were a major form of entertainment. Mature adult bands provided isolated communities with an important kind of recreation. Many community activities were heralded by the official presence of music organizations which frequently became a rallying point for civic interest and pride.

In many communities, the merchants furnished financial backing by contributing a few dollars each month to support the band. Additional money was raised by community sponsored rummage sales, ice cream socials, and other renumerative activities. In the state of Iowa, Major George W. Landers was able to promote successfully a five mill band tax for the support of community bands.

In return for this support, the bands usually played free outdoor concerts during the summer months. To prepare for these concerts, one or two evenings a week, both summer and winter, were devoted to rehearsals. Bandstands were erected in parks and town squares and families gathered on weekends to hear the summer concerts and to visit with neighbors.

Times have changed! As the American public turned more and more to the radio, the phonograph, and the movies for entertainment, the interest of adult members in the community bands diminished and young people began filling the vacant chairs left by their elders. It was this surge of interest in the band program by young America which ultimately brought instrumental music into the public schools.

Public School Instrumental Music

Following the early lead of the adult orchestras and bands, public school music in America has always emphasized performance. At first, youth music groups were organized outside the school. Gradually, bands and orchestras became a recognized part of the school program. The pattern described by W. Otto Miessner was duplicated in many communities.

> One day we told the boys that we, with their cooperation, would organize a brass band. At first they were incredulous, then grew interested. It was explained to them that the better a boy's attitude toward the regular music work, the better his chances for acceptance into the band membership . . . I arranged for fifteen minute lesson periods with the boys whose parents had consented to buy instruments. These lessons I gave during the noon intermission and after school hours, and within two months I had twelve boys, which number soon increased to eighteen, all of whom I taught individually and in ensemble in this manner . . . This year (1909) the number has been increased to 32 pieces with instruments worth in the aggregate over $12,000 . . . A number of these boys come from the various grade buildings in order to stimulate an interest in the grades . . . The age of the present members ranges from eleven to seventeen years (Theodore F. Normann, *Instrumental Music in the Public Schools*, Oliver Ditson Co., 1941, p. 15, quoting W. Otto in an article in *School Music*, March, 1909.)

America still looked to Europe for leadership and since there was no precedent in England, France, or Germany for instrumental music in the schools, there was some hesitancy about including it in the regular curriculum. However, adolescent boys and girls continued to join youth bands and orchestras and there was mounting pressure from parents to make the rehearsals part of the school day.

Orchestras were the first to gain entry. By 1910, there were over 100 orchestras organized as a part of public school programs. Bands gained acceptance shortly thereafter. Veteran bandsmen, returning home with musical training and experience from playing in the Army and Navy bands of World War I, became the teachers and directors for school bands. "Class instruction," a new teaching technique pioneered in England, gave these men a tool with which to mold beginning instrumentalists into bands. During the decade between 1920 and 1930, instrumental music found a place in the public school curriculum.

17

To meet the continuing demand for instrumental teachers, colleges hastened to develop courses for training instrumental teachers. In 1923, Fred Innes, a famous trombone virtuoso, established the National School of Music in Chicago to train band directors. The expansion of school music programs and the scarcity of band directors to meet increased demands encouraged hundreds of ambitious students to enroll in his school. Instrument manufacturers and uniform companies gave additional support to the band movement.

Instrumental music entered the public schools not as an academic subject, but as a dynamic program geared to train musicians to participate in performing groups. Thus, a unique characteristic of music in American public schools is that it has been *performance* oriented. The emphasis has been on music *making.* From the beginning, public school music programs have been directed toward teaching young people to *perform* as vocalists or instrumentalists.

Competition and Public School Music

Attending district, regional, and state music contests for marching and concert bands is an accepted part of most school band programs. In the sample of bands studied, 42% of the large high schools and 51% of the small high schools reported participation in marching band contests. Participation is even higher in concert band contests and festivals where 76% of the large schools and 81% of the small schools compete in such events.

Competition is not limited to large groups but also includes as many small ensembles and soloists as the band director is able to organize and coach. The typical high school band director prepares 13.2 ensembles for competition each year. There are a few schools that do not have any ensemble program. At the other extreme, there were three directors who reported preparing 50 ensembles for their yearly contests, two who prepared 45, and five who prepared between 40 and 45. Of all the band directors interviewed, 27% had prepared 20 or more ensembles for contest during the year, in addition to their work with large groups.

Soloists require almost as much director time and assistance as ensembles. The typical high school director coached 21.5 soloists for contests but four directors said they worked with over 100 students and another worked with 85. Of the directors interviewed, 24 per cent reported that they had worked with 30 or more soloists.

There are striking regional differences in participation in solo and ensemble contests. Southern directors are the most active. They coach an average of 28.4 soloists and 18.4 ensembles. Midwestern directors are close behind with 26.5 soloists and 18.5 ensembles. Directors from the Great Lakes region work with the same number of soloists as those from the Midwest, 26.5, but have slightly fewer ensembles, 16.0. Pacific Coast directors are much less active in this area, coaching an average of 10.3 soloists and 5.2 ensembles.

The Roots of Public School Music Competition

The roots of the competitive performance orientation of American public school music are also historical. Music in the early American colonies was mainly vocal. One of the earliest music groups was a singing class of 48 members which met in 1774 at the home of Robert Capen in Stoughten, Massachusetts. By 1786, this singing class, directed by William Billings, had developed into the first American music organization for which we have historical records — the Stoughten Musical Society. Other communities followed and there were soon additional societies in Canton and Sharon.

The multiplication of music societies led to the first music contest, held shortly after the Revolutionary War. This contest was instigated and encouraged by the clergy. Louis C. Elson describes the event:

> . . . Many clergymen, in following the good old fashion of "exchanging pulpits," had become familiar with the excellent church music of Stoughten, and sounded its praises abroad. The singers of the First Parish of Dorchester, Massachusetts took umbrage at this, and challenged the Stoughten vocalists to a trail of skill. The gauntlet was at once taken up, and the contest took place in a large hall in Dorchester, many of the leading Bostonians coming out to witness it. The Dorchester choristers were male and female, and had the assistance of a bass viol. The Stoughten party consisted of twenty selected male voices, without instruments, led by the president of the Stoughten Musical Society, Elijah Dunbar, a man of dignified presence and of excellent voice. The Dorchester singers began with a new anthem. The Stoughtenians commenced with Jacob French's "Heavenly Vision", the author of which was their fellow townsman. When they finally sang, without books, Handel's "Hallelujah Chorus" the Dorchestrians gave up the contest, and gracefully acknowledged defeat . . . (Louis C. Elson, *The History of American Music*, New York: Macmillan)

That first vocal contest in post-Revolutionary War Massachusetts between competing church choirs was typically American. It set the tone for much that was to follow.

The Pressures of Preparing for Performances

With the blueprint of performance and competition indelibly etched on the music departments of America, band, orchestra, and choir directors continue to multiply performances until today the typical band director is giving 14.5 performances in a school year, prepares 13.2 ensembles for competition, and coaches 21.5 soloists for contest. Of course, these band performances are not spread evenly throughout the school year — halftime shows come in the fall, and music contests usually come in the spring. If they were evenly distributed, however, the typical band director would be responsible for about 50 public performances per school year — more than five per month.

When a band director is expected to present a major performance every other week and to prepare numerous ensembles and soloists for contest, it is readily apparent that there are not enough hours in the school day in which to hold the necessary rehearsals and to give the necessary lessons. Extra rehearsals and long working days are a way of life for the public school band director.

Marching Band

The pressures on band directors are particularly onerous during the marching band season. The first football game is ordinarily scheduled for a few days after school opens in the fall, and there is little time to organize the band before the first game unless, of course, band rehearsals begin before school opens. Preseason rehearsals are not uncommon. Home games are usually scheduled one or two weeks apart and the home crowd expects a new spectacular at every football game.

Twenty-two (out of 222) directors whom I visited have found a solution to their football halftime problems — *they have abolished the marching band!* However, only a few directors have this option. For most, the training of a marching band is an integral part of their assignment and they have no alternative but to hold extra rehearsals to meet the performance demands. Thus, they schedule extra rehearsals before school, after school, and in the evening in a frantic attempt to satisfy performance demands.

Most of the high school marching bands in the study met for a 55-minute period five times a week during the school day, although there were 10 bands which met only four times a week; 13 that met three times a week; and three that met only twice a week during school hours. Apparently, this is not sufficient time to prepare intricate halftime shows. There were 183 marching band directors who answered the questions about marching band, and 141 of them (77%) reported holding extra out-of-school rehearsals during marching season. On an average, these 183 marching band directors held 1.9 extra rehearsals per week. Some directors are very demanding on themselves and their students. Three directors reported holding 10 extra rehearsals a week — five in the morning before school and five after school! Eight others hold rehearsals either before or after school every day *and* one or two evenings a week; twenty-six hold five extra rehearsals a week, either before or after school; and 78 hold one or two evening rehearsals a week, another reported rehearsing four evenings a week, and two reported rehearsing three evenings. All four of these directors were nominated for their outstanding departments!

Overall, however, directors who spend long hours in extra rehearsals with their marching bands were not nominated more often by the university judges than those who did not. In fact, during marching season, the non-nominated directors average 2.6 rehearsals a week to 2.3 for the nominated directors. As we will see later, this is because university judges do not give much weight to marching band performance in evaluating music departments.

However, when we correlated extra marching band rehearsals with the number of marching contests won by the band, there was a significant relationship — those directors who held the most rehearsals tended to win the most contests. Directors who had won no marching band contests reported an average of 1.6 extra rehearsals per week while those who had won one contest reported 2.4 extra rehearsals and those who had won two or more contests reported an average of 2.9 extra rehearsals per week. These differences are statistically significant. Although the general relationship is clear, an individual band director may be holding many extra rehearsals and still not be winning marching contests. Two of the directors holding 10 extra rehearsals a week won *no* marching contests and many who rehearsed five and six times a week were in the "no-win" category. In general, however, those who held more extra rehearsals won more marching contests.

It appears that two extra rehearsals a week are necessary if a band director is to meet his halftime show commitments. More rehearsals are generally required of those who wish to win marching band contests as well.

Concert Bands

Most concert bands meet five periods a week during school hours, but there were exceptions. In five extreme cases, directors reported that their concert bands are not given any rehearsal time during the regular school day and always met outside of school.

Many directors who hold extra rehearsals during the fall marching season stop holding them during concert season. Only 55% of the band directors in this study hold rehearsals in non-school hours during concert season, a drop of 22% from marching season. But, those directors who do hold extra rehearsals call even more rehearsals than during marching season: 51 directors hold five extra rehearsals a week, 11 hold six extra rehearsals, one holds seven extra rehearsals, 12 hold 10 extra rehearsals and one holds 11 extra rehearsals. The director holding 11 rehearsals was meeting his group every morning before school, every afternoon after school, and one evening a week! These 76 directors holding five or more rehearsals a week represent 36% of the directors who answered the question.

Do extra rehearsals pay off in a performance-oriented system? The answer is both "yes" and "no." The 55% who hold extra rehearsals were not any more likely to be nominated by the university judges than those who do not hold extra rehearsals. Nominated bands had an additional 2.8 rehearsals every week to 2.6 rehearsals for the matched bands.This difference is insignificant. Thus, extra rehearsals, alone, do not ensure that a department will be regarded as outstanding by university judges.

On the other hand, those who hold more rehearsals do go significantly further past the district level in concert band competition. The average number of rehearsals per week was identical for bands that received first division rating and bands that did not receive a first division rating in district competition. But, the bands that went beyond district competition practice significantly more often — 4.4 times per week. Also, concert bands which won more first division ratings were likely to be considered outstanding by the university judges. University judges are sensitive to ratings in concert band competition but not to ratings won in marching band competition. The typical band director holds approximately two extra rehearsals a week during marching season and closer to three extra rehearsals a week during concert season. Those who wish to win marching contests and to get beyond the district in concert band contests must work even harder. It is very difficult to be a success in a performance-dominated system with five rehearsals a week; however, most directors indicated that they thoroughly enjoy the activities of their profession.

Summary

In this chapter we have reviewed briefly the historic origin of performance-oriented public school music. We have seen how performance responsibilities have so multiplied that directors are giving an average of 1.5 performances a month during the school year as well as preparing 13.2 ensembles for competition. Sandwiched in between these large and small group performances, the typical high school band director is coaching 21.5 soloists.

Although these performances are not spread evenly throughout the school year, the results are the same. The typical band director is responsible for 50 public performances each 9 1/2 months (the average school year) — over 5 per month. To meet the heavy demands of performance, directors are unable to find adequate time during regular school hours to rehearse. During the fall, preseason rehearsals are common and as school opens, directors schedule extra rehearsals before school, after school, and in the evening in their effort to meet the expectations of football fans.

As the season changes from outside performance to concerts and contests held indoors, 55% of the band directors continue to hold rehearsals before school, after school, and in the evening. Thus we see that performances and rehearsals have become a way of life for the high school band director.

Chapter III

Performance and Its Price

Attend any music educators convention and you will find band directors leaving the convention hall laden with chocolate bars, fruit-cake, bags of candy, shoe polish, seat cushions, ballpoint pens, light bulbs, pencils, toothbrushes, and Christmas tree decorations. These are samples of products designed to produce a quick profit when huckstering teenagers and parents join forces with their band director to raise money to support the instrumental program. The booths for such promoters are sandwiched in between the educational displays, part of the customary panoply of the music educator convention.

It was only as I analyzed the data from the interviews that I learned, to my amazement, that the band directors in the 197 schools in my sample raised a total of over a half-million dollars during the school year in which I visited them — a feat carried out while holding two extra rehearsals per week and staging a performance every other week. The total amount earned was $580,888 or an average of almost $3,000 per director. Figure 2 describes the source and average amount raised by instrumental departments in various regions and for the sample as a whole.

Southern directors raise significantly more money than directors in other regions, an average of $4,523 per school. Directors in the Great Lakes region are next with an average of $3,559; Midwestern directors are considerably lower with $2,576 per school; and Pacific Coast directors rank last with an average of $2,274. The directors in the South are raising twice as much money as those on the Pacific Coast. But, in either case, the totals are truly remarkable.

Six major sources of outside income are reported by directors. Nationally, the largest amount of revenue is contributed by band booster groups. About 43% of the additional income is earned by parents; 25% is earned through special projects originating with the director and involving his students; and 20% comes from receipts from ticket sales to programs and concerts. These three sources account for 88% of the total funds raised. These are not levies against the music student. However, the other three sources of income derive either di-

Figure 2

SOURCES OF ADDITIONAL INCOME —
NATIONAL AVERAGE AND BY REGIONS

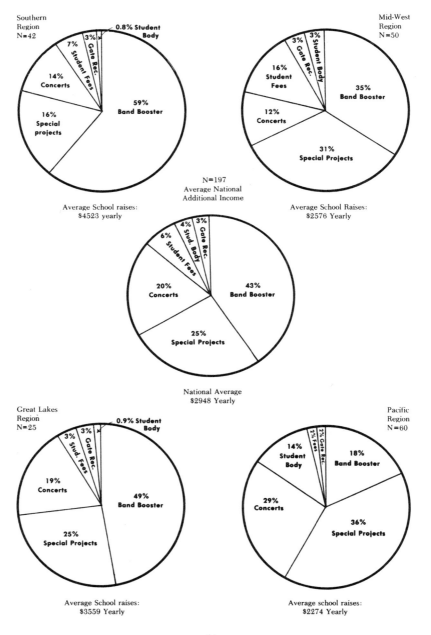

Southern
Region
N=42

0.8% Student Body
3% Gate Rec.
7% Student Fees
14% Concerts
16% Special projects
59% Band Booster

Average School raises:
$4523 yearly

Mid-West
Region
N=50

3% Gate Rec.
3% Student Body
16% Student Fees
35% Band Booster
12% Concerts
31% Special Projects

Average School Raises:
$2576 Yearly

N=197
Average National
Additional Income

3% Gate Rec.
3% Stud. Body
4% Student Fees
6%
20% Concerts
43% Band Booster
25% Special Projects

National Average
$2948 Yearly

Great Lakes
Region
N=25

0.9% Student Body
3% Gate Rec.
3% Stud. Fees
19% Concerts
49% Band Booster
25% Special Projects

Average School raises:
$3559 Yearly

Pacific
Region
N=60

2% Gate Rec.
2% Fees
14% Student Body
18% Band Booster
29% Concerts
36% Special Projects

Average school raises:
$2274 Yearly

24

rectly or indirectly from the students and their parents; the student laboratory fee (6%) is a direct charge; student body funds (4%) constitute an indirect charge; and contributions from gate receipts at athletic events (3%) may be either a direct or indirect charge, depending on the school policy. Most directors are reluctant to charge their students music fees and so they secure supplementary funds from other sources.

Figure 2 shows that not only the amount of money but also its source varies from region to region. Southern band directors, who raise the largest amount of supplementary money, also report receiving more help from their band booster clubs than directors in other regions; 59% of their money is produced by parents. The Great Lakes directors report 49% of their additional income contributed by band booster activities; Midwestern directors report 35% and Pacific Coast directors report only 18%. The more the band boosters are involved, the more money a band director is likely to have to operate his department.

Nationally, the second most important source of additional income (25%) is from special projects initiated by the director himself. Pacific Coast directors, who make least use of booster clubs, depend more heavily (36%) on special projects. The Midwestern directors rank second on special projects with 31%, followed by the Great Lakes directors with 25%, and Southern directors with only 16% coming from special projects. In these projects, the burden rests mainly upon the director. He must organize his instrumental students to sell the kinds of products promoted at conventions. He is fully involved in the mechanics of raising money to support his program.

Only a small amount of the additional income is produced by concert receipts. This percentage varies slightly from region to region. Pacific Coast directors, who have the lowest total income, report a high of 29% followed by the Great Lakes directors with 19%, Southern directors with 14% and the Midwestern directors with only 12%. Student fees, athletic gate receipts, and funds from the student body contribute only about 13% of the total. Midwestern band directors make almost 16% of their additional income from student assessments, but this is a very minor source of income in every other region. Contributions from student body fees are significant only on the Pacific Coast (14%).

As noted in Chapter 2, performance demands are practically the same regardless of the size of the school. Consequently, the cost of running an instrumental program is approximately the same whether one is teaching in a large school or a small school. It is not surprising to find that there is no significant difference between the amount of extra money which the directors in small and large high schools must earn to support their programs. On an average, the large high school director augments his yearly regular school budget by $3,099 compared to $2,819 earned by the small school director. The small high school band leans more heavily on band boosters for support (50%) than do large high schools (39%). Both acquire approximately one-fourth of their additional income from special projects led by the director. Large schools receive proportionately more of their outside income from concert receipts, student body fees, student laboratory fees, and athletic gate receipts.

There were only 10 band directors (5% of those interviewed) who reported operating their programs without money beyond that provided in the regular school budget — seven were nominated bands and three were in the matched group. In other words, 95% of the band programs in my study required financing beyond that provided by the school district.

In addition to the 10 directors who raised no additional money, there were nine directors who reported that their only additional funds were student body fees, athletic gate receipts, and music student (laboratory) fees. These sources of revenue do not require non-educational activities on the part of the director. At the other extreme, I found four directors who had to raise the *entire* budget for their department themselves! The school provided no money for instruments, repairs, music, uniforms, or any expense beyond the salary of the director. Fortunately, this situation is not widespread.

Of the 205 directors who answered the question about source of additional revenue, 186 or 90.7% reported they were earning operational funds themselves through ticket sales, special projects, and parent groups. Forty-two per cent of the directors interviewed had at least one special selling project during that school year. This does not count similar events which may have been sponsored by their parent groups. Fifty-one per cent of the directors had booster clubs; 20% had both special projects and booster clubs.

It is interesting to note that the directors nominated for their outstanding departments were able to supplement their budgets by an average of $3,323 compared to the non-nominated directors who raised an average of $2,643. For most directors, both nominated and matched, performance has a price.

Other Kinds of Price

When I visited the band directors in my study, I asked them the number of students enrolled in their band programs and the number of students enrolled in the high school. I found that there were 22,657 students actively engaged in the band programs in the high schools I studied and these schools enrolled a total of 308,492 students. This means that only 7.41 per cent of all the students in the schools visited are enrolled in band.

The American School Band Directors Association made a study of 369 schools. It found that the typical public school band in America has 93 members, 51 boys and 42 girls, and is located in a school with an average enrollment of 1,260 students. If we divide 93 by 1,260, we find that 7.38% of the students in the schools in this survey are participating in band, a percentage almost identical to that found in my survey. The ASBDA estimated another 10 to 12% of the student body might be participating in orchestra or vocal music classes.(Unpublished report of the Committee on Band Uniform Survey of the American School Band Directors Association, conducted by the Marketing Research Department, Raeford Worsted Company, Division of Burlington Industries, Walter Lake, Chairman. Homer Anderson, Bardwell Donaldson, Donald Stump, 1965.) If we use that optimistic estimate, we would conclude that approximately 20% of the students in these schools may be receiving some music education. On the other hand, there are at least 80% of the students in these high schools who are probably receiving little or no music education.

There are some slight regional differences. Midwestern schools include 9.2% of their student bodies in instrumental music; the South, 9%; the Great Lakes states, 7%; and the Pacific Coast schools, 6.5%. Although these differences appear small, they *are* statistically significant. Schools in the South and the Midwest provide a music education for more of their high school students than schools in either the Great Lakes area or the Pacific Coast area. However, no region involves as much as 10% of its students in the band program.

The larger the high school, the larger the band, but the smaller the percentage of students who take instrumental music. Figure 3 is a bar chart showing the percentage of large and small high schools with various sized instrumental programs. Twenty-five per cent of the large high schools have bands with less than 100 members; 42% have 100 to 149 members; 24% have 150 to 199 members; and 9% have over 200 instrumentalists. When we combine both nominated and matched schools, the average large high school has 133 students in its program and 1,993 in the student body.

Seventy-four per cent of the small high schools have bands with under 100 members; 19% have 100 to 149 students; 5% have 150 to 199; and only 2% have 200 or more bandsmen. The average small high school has 89 members and 699 students in the student body. Thus we see that instrumental music in our high schools is serving only a small percentage of our students.

The Price Paid by Ethnic Minority Groups

The same selective process which recruits only 7.4% of the student body of the average high school into the band program also operates

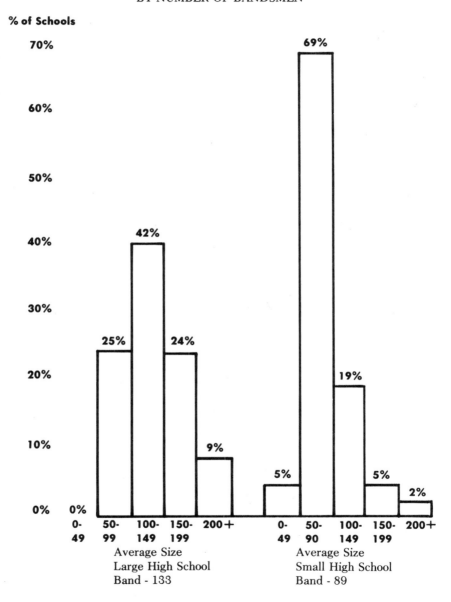

Figure 3

COMPARISON OF LARGE AND SMALL HIGH SCHOOL BANDS
BY NUMBER OF BANDSMEN

% of Schools

Average Size
Large High School
Band - 133

Average Size
Small High School
Band - 89

to select fewer children from cultural and ethnic minorities into the program than would be expected from their proportion in the high high school population.

Although Negroes have contributed a great deal to the American music heritage, relatively few Negro children are involved in band programs in the public schools. For each school visited, I learned the percentage of Negroes in the total student body and the percentage of Negroes in the instrumental program. From these replies, we can estimate that there were 12,771 Negro students enrolled in the schools in the sample and approximately 507 Negro bandsmen in the 194 band programs for which I had the necessary information. This indicates that 4.1% of the students in the sample schools are Negro. Approximately 10% of the population of the United States is Negro. This means that there is an underrepresentation of Negroes in the schools nominated as having outstanding bands and in the geographic neighbors with which they were matched. Only 2.2% of the students in the sample band programs are Negroes, about half as many Negro students as we would expect if they were represented according to their proportion in the total student population of sample schools.

In the South, about 6.4% of the students in the high schools visited were Negro while 3.6% of the students in band were Negro. In the Great Lakes area, comparable percentages were 5.7 and 3.1; in the Midwest, 4.5 and 2.9; on the Pacific Coast, 4.5 and 3.4%. None of these differences between regions is statistically significant. In general, schools enroll only slightly more than half as many Negro students in instrumental music as would be expected if Negroes were represented in proportion to their numbers in the school population. No predominantly Negro high schools were nominated as having outstanding instrumental departments.

Large high schools are doing a better job of involving black students in their band programs than small high schools; 6% of the students in the large high schools visited are Negro, and 4% of them are in band. In small high schools, 2.5% of the students were Negro, but only .5% of them participated in band.

The nationwide figures for participation of Mexican-American students are very similar to those for Negro students. About 4.2% of the students in the high schools visited were Mexican-Americans, but only 2.6% of the students in the instrumental programs were Mexican-American. Mexican-American students are concentrated in the Southern and Pacific Coast regions. In Texas and Florida, Mexican-American children make up 12.3% of the high schools visited; about 8.4% of the students were in their bands. On the Pacific Coast, 4.4% of the student population in the schools visited was Mexican-American, but only 2.1% of the students were in band. About half the number of Pacific Coast Mexican-American students are enrolled as would be expected from their proportion in the population while in the South, about three-fourths of the expected number are enrolled. It appears that Texas and Florida are doing a better job of encouraging Mexican-American students to participate in instrumental music than the Pacific states. The Great Lakes region with only 1% Mexican-Americans and the Midwest with .9% have approximately the anticipated number of Mexican-American children in their bands.

Participation in band can be especially important to a student from a minority background. Several years ago a robust young Mexican-American joined my band as a junior in high school. Juan quickly learned to play the sousaphone and was elected sergeant for the sousaphone rank in his senior year. In this position, he served on the band legislative committee and the council of officers which reviews disciplinary cases. For the first time in high school, Juan felt that he was playing a significant role in the school. His senior year was climaxed by the band's appearance in the Los Angeles Coliseum during the N.F.L. All-Star Pro-Bowl Game.

Following graduation, Juan enlisted in the Marines as a paratrooper and was soon in overseas combat. He wrote frequent letters to the band and, after almost two years of fighting, returned to visit me one evening — on crutches. He told me that one night he had been dropped deep in enemy territory. Confused by the darkness, he misjudged his timing and landed in a tree, seriously injuring himself. When he regained consciousness, he found himself swinging in the tree with an enemy patrol moving up the hill in his direction. Helpless paratroopers are prime targets and Juan tried desperately to free himself but the pain was too intense. At this point, he heard the sound of small arms fire. The enemy patrol disappeared into the brush, and he heard someone calling his name. He looked down to find a patrol of his buddies who quickly freed him and radioed for a helicopter. As the helicopter lifted from the ground, bullets from the underbrush ripped through the floor and one hit Juan in the spine as he lay strapped on a stretcher.

Doctors at the base hospital managed to save Juan's life but, after several weeks, were convinced he would never walk again. Juan told me how his thoughts had turned repeatedly to the two wonderful years he had had in band. As he lay in bed, he relived the parades, the concerts, the officers' meetings and the big performance in the coliseum. Reflecting on happier times when he had marched with his sousaphone, he vowed that he would not be crippled but would return to visit the band. The day after he visited my home, Juan walked into the music room. He visited several of the classes of his former teachers to tell the students about his experiences and how the bright memories of his days in the band had helped him through his time of despair.

Other music directors, no doubt, can provide similar experiences where a "minority" student gained much through participation in music.

The Price Paid in Selective Recruiting

Many of the high school band directors interviewed are not responsible for the initial recruitment of instrumentalists because this takes place in the elementary schools. Therefore, I could not inquire about the policies which govern the selection of beginning instrumentalists. However, it is common practice in many elementary schools to give musical aptitude tests to eliminate children with little natural talent for music performance. Those who pass the test are encouraged to become beginning instrumentalists while those who do not will probably receive little, if any, instrumental music education. Ordinarily, the number of beginning players is limited by finances and by the amount of time the instrumental teacher has to spend in each school. Only the talented, according to the aptitude test, are recruited. Thus, the future instrumental music education of children between nine and 12 years of age hinges heavily on their performance on an aptitude test or on a screening interview conducted in the elementary school. Unfortunately, these screening devices are frequently unreliable.

One director told me about a boy who had failed his screening test but, without consulting the teacher, had proceeded to buy a snare drum with the money he made from his paper route. Although skeptical, the director enrolled him in the beginning percussion class where he proceeded to eclipse the efforts of the other young drummers who had ranked higher on the particular music aptitude test used. At the end of the first year, he moved from the beginning drum class into the junior high school band, and, at the end of his senior year in high school, received the highest award given by the band department. Later, the director learned that this boy was a non-reader. He had failed the music aptitude test because he could not read the directions. However, his inability to read words did not interfere with his reading music.

Pressures for quality performance eliminate children who have special physical handicaps because there is not enough time to permit experimentation. Several years ago I was judging a solo and ensemble contest in a small town in northern Iowa. It was about two o'clock in the afternoon and I was slightly behind schedule. When the next soloist stepped to the piano and tuned his instrument, I had not completely finished writing the comments on the previous performer. I motioned for the waiting trombonist to begin and finished my written remarks while listening to the solo without looking at the soloist. Impressed by what I heard, I set aside the adjudication sheet and looked carefully at the young performer. He was holding his trombone in a most unusual manner. His left elbow was pushed far to the right of his body and underneath the slide. This position permitted his left hand to hold the instrument near the mouthpiece and to rest against his face. His left thumb and index finger pinched his nose in a most unorthodox fashion. But the tone coming from the instrument was mature and the technique excellent. It was the finest trombone performance of the day.

When the young man finished, I learned that he had been playing trombone for three years. He attended a very small high school and the music teacher knew little about instrumental music. She had started him on trombone because it was the only instrument in the school that was not being used. His harelip and soft palate had caused difficulty at first but he learned that he could direct the air through the mouthpiece instead of having it come out through his nostrils if he held his nose with his left hand. This boy would have failed most physical and music aptitude tests.

Even if the child passes the aptitude test, he must be self-motivated to accept the invitation to start playing an instrument and, frequently, must have parents who are willing to purchase or rent an instrument for him to play. Many districts do not provide instruments for beginners, so that parental financial resources become a third selection factor. A primary factor limiting the participation of children from minority families and disadvantaged backgrounds is undoubtedly the financial cost of investing in an instrument. Even if parents can afford an instrument, a major task of the elementary instrumental teacher is selling parents and children on making the investment.

Only those few children who survive these three selective processes — aptitude tests, interest, and financial ability — will become beginning instrumentalists. Is it any wonder that such a small percentage of children in the public school receive an instrumental music education?

This stringent screening process produces remarkable uniformity from one district to the next. In my study, I found that the average junior high school each year sends 23 students to large high schools, while the junior high schools feeding small high schools send an average of 25 students a year. By the end of the ninth grade, the selection process is already complete and the musical elite already established.

The Price Paid in Drop-Outs

Only 10.6% of the high schools surveyed have a program for beginners. This means that, in most schools, a child who is not recruited for instrumental music in the elementary or junior high will not have the opportunity to enter the program later in his education. From a performance orientation, this policy is reasonable. It takes a long time for a child to become a proficient performer on an instrument and a student who first begins playing in high school is unlikely to be of much value as a performer in his high school band or orchestra. Therefore, performance orientation makes the development of beginning instrumental programs at the high school level undesirable.

Because there is no augmentation of the instrumental music program during the high school years, the program can only experience attrition and the inclusion of a smaller and smaller proportion of the students in each grade as students progress from freshmen to seniors. The typical high school has 22 12th grade bandsmen. It is significant that large three-year high schools report more seniors (33) than large four-year high schools (20). The same is true for small high schools but the differences are not so large (20 as compared to 17). Figure 4 shows the drop-out rate comparing three and four-year high schools. All the differences between three and four-year schools are statistically significant. The large three-year high school has 50 bandsmen in 10th grade, 42 in 11th, and 33 in 12th compared to 35, 31, and 20 in four-year high schools. The small three-year high school has 33, 30, and 20 bandsmen in each successive grade while the small four-year high school has 26, 20, and 17 bandsmen in grades 10, 11, and 12.

These differences in attrition are directly related to the performance-oriented philosophy of the public schools. The size of the instrumental program is determined by the number of musicians the director feels will provide an adequate instrumentation for both outdoor and indoor performances. If the desired number is 100 bandsmen, then there must be enough bandsmen in each grade to fill this instrumentation. Thus, the four-year high school can average 25 band members in each grade and have a 100-piece band but the three-year high school must average 33. These are almost exactly the numbers which we found as averages in the survey. This would explain why the three-year high school consistently has a larger number of bandsmen in each grade. The ceiling is determined by performance needs, not by student demand or educational philosophy or what participation in band might mean to a student.

Summary

This chapter has established that performance has its price — in money and in the number of young people who are able or unable to participate in the band program. The performance orientation of public school music appears to be the primary factor in the selection process. When an instrumental program is large enough to meet the needs of the high school for performing groups, there is an automatic ceiling on the number of students who will be included. Most high

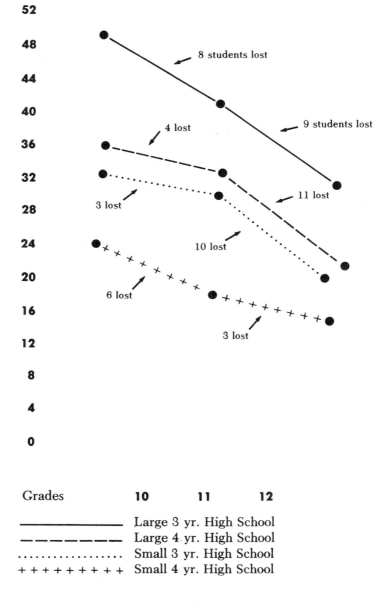

Figure 4

COMPARISON OF THE THREE AND FOUR YEAR HIGH
SCHOOLS BY THE NUMBER OF BAND MEMBERS
REPORTED IN EACH CLASS

8 students lost

4 lost

9 students lost

3 lost

11 lost

10 lost

6 lost

3 lost

Grades   10   11   12

——————————— Large 3 yr. High School
— — — — — — — Large 4 yr. High School
.... Small 3 yr. High School
+ + + + + + + + Small 4 yr. High School

34

schools have one band director regardless of the size of the student body. Four-year high schools involve proportionately fewer students than three-year high schools because they have an additional grade to draw upon. The composition of the elite is established in elementary school through selective recruiting in which the talented, motivated, and financially able are favored. There is almost no replacement of drop-outs at the high school level. Therefore, the number of instrumental music students declines progressively as students move through school. Performance has dictated the number of students who will receive an instrumental music education and the price is high.

Chapter IV

The Promoters

If a band director expects to hold two or three extra rehearsals per week and must raise two or three thousand dollars a year to finance his performances, then it is imperative that he develop support for his department among other faculty members, his school administration, the students, and the community. His colleagues and parents must be willing to tolerate the extra rehearsals and both parents and community must be willing to contribute time and money to his fund-raising ventures.

Thus each band director must work adroitly to maximize his support while minimizing frictions. If he pushes too hard, his administration and parents may find him too difficult and too demanding. If he does not push hard enough, he cannot compete in the performance-oriented world of public school music.

Most band directors are aware of this rather delicate balance and realize that their role in the performance-oriented system requires yet another type of skill totally unrelated to music education — skill in promoting support for the program among the faculty, the administration, and the community.

Does a director have to be a "winner" in music competition to have faculty support? The answer to this question is very clear in the data — a director does *not* have to win acclaim in the competitive world of school bands to have his faculty behind him. There is no evidence in my data that faculty or administrations, in general, are pressing directors to win trophies and first division ratings. Of course, there are always exceptions.

Certain situational factors, over which the band director has little control, *do* influence the amount of faculty support he is likely to receive. Directors who report a high level of staff support are significantly more likely to be teaching in small high schools. Apparently the intimacy of the small group increases feelings of mutuality and cooperation. In addition, directors who enjoy high faculty support are more likely to be men who report that the music department was at a low ebb when they were initially employed by the school. Evidently, other staff members are more supportive when the music department is in disarray and the new director faces the task of organizing an effective program. If the director reports that the program was already good or excellent when he arrived, other teachers are less likely to rally to his support. Staff support is also significantly greater in schools which are in high school districts that have only one or two other high schools. Directors in the metropolitan district schools report significantly less backing from fellow faculty members.

Other factors which differentiate directors with high faculty support from those with low support are more closely under the director's personal control. It takes time to promote the interpersonal relations which lead to high support. Therefore it is not surprising to find that the directors who report enjoying the highest staff support have been teaching longer in their schools — an average of 11.3 years compared to 8.6 years for directors reporting low support.

However, time alone does not build support for a department. Time can just as easily erode support if there are abrasive encounters between the director and staff over the years. Therefore I examined some of the attitudes of the director which might be related to building the desired support. Directors who believe that the primary purpose of the instrumental music program is to develop discipline and responsibility in students have less staff support than directors with broader educational goals. Interestingly enough, directors who are teaching classes other than instrumental music enjoy less support than those who specialize entirely in their own field. Directors whose students receive instrumental lessons *during* school hours enjoy *less* staff support because the more disruptions there are in academic class schedules, the lower the staff backing.

Another factor which decreases faculty support is the attitude of the director toward his work. Directors who believe they should receive commissions on instruments purchased by their students and who feel that they should not be expected to put in extra hours without being paid for them were significantly less likely to enjoy the support of their fellow faculty members. On the other hand, directors who were hard workers, who were willing to accept invitations to perform on weekends, who did not expect to be paid for every extra hour of work, and who were willing to work after school with their students, enjoyed significantly greater support from fellow faculty members. In addition, the directors who enjoyed the most faculty support were significantly more likely to report that they were "very satisfied" with their jobs.

Probably the most significant factor in gaining the support of other faculty members was the director's view of his place on the faculty team. Directors who enjoy the esteem of other faculty members were more likely to believe that a student should not jeopardize his academic grades by practicing too much on his instrument, to believe that winning trophies is less important than amicable relations with other teachers, and to believe that the instrumental department should not insist on having the football field for practice over the objections of the athletic department. They also believe that a director should not push so hard in trying to win contests that he makes other teachers angry. Directors who report the highest staff support were significantly more likely to express cooperative attitudes.

One might expect that a director who is hard working and not self-seeking, who sees himself as a member of the faculty team rather than a *prima donna,* and who cooperates with the school administration should enjoy more faculty support. But how does this affect his program? Do these cooperative attitudes interfere with his success as a band director? Apparently not. Directors who were highly rated by the university judges were more likely to report friction with the physical education department, but, beyond that, there were no differences. A director's attitudes toward his fellow faculty members and his job were not related to the number of marching or concert band contests he won, nor to the average rating he received from the university judges. Thus, the cooperative director is not penalized for his agreeable attitudes but neither is he rewarded for them.

I had thought that the total number of rehearsals held by a director might influence the amount of staff support he reports; but I found that the number of rehearsals makes no difference. The average number of extra marching band rehearsals in high support schools was 1.78 compared with 1.97 in low support schools. The average number of extra concert band rehearsals in high support schools was 2.7 compared to 2.6 in low support schools. Clearly, it is not so much the actual demands for time made by the director as it is his general attitude toward other staff members which determines the extent to which they support the instrumental program.

Promoting Support in the Community

Does a director have to be a "winner" to enjoy high community support? In this case, the answer is equivocable. A director does not have to be highly regarded by university judges to enjoy support in his own community. There were just as many bands in the high support group which were not nominated by the university judges as bands who were nominated. The high support directors did not win any more marching band contests. But, there was a correlation between the number of first division concert band ratings and community support when the entire sample of 197 bands was studied. The more first division ratings for concert playing, the more community support. Of course, we cannot tell whether high community support helps to produce an excellent performing group or whether an excellent performing group generates high community support. All we can say is that the two are related; one helps the other.

As with faculty support, there are certain situational factors which characterize communities which give strong backing to the instrumental program: 1. a strong relationship between the size of school and community backing — the larger the school, the *less* the backing; 2. the more high schools in the district, the less the community backing; 3. the greater the number of years a director has taught in the community, the greater the amount of support. Directors in new high schools also reported significantly less community support than teachers in well-established schools. Community support was also significantly lower when directors were teaching other subjects in addition to instrumental music. It may be that the director who must prepare to teach academic subjects is not able to give the same time and attention to the instrumental program as one whose total commitment is to instrumental music. This divided attention tends to reduce the amount of community backing. The director who rates his instrumental department as having been in poor condition when he first assumed direction is more likely to have high community support just as he is more likely to have high faculty support. If he takes over a department in good or excellent condition, he has more difficulty building support for his program both from the community and from the staff.

Promoting Student Support

A series of questions evaluated the amount of student support reported by each director. Directors reported that student support is closely related to the number of first division ratings the concert band receives. The more first division ratings, the more student support. The student body is less likely to support the director who sees his primary purpose as building responsibility and discipline in his band members, and the director who emphasizes the dollar and cents payoff he should receive for his work. However, they do support the director who is willing to work hard. Unlike staff and community support, student support was not related to the size of the school, or the number of high schools in the district, or whether the director teaches other subjects, or the number of years he has taught in his present school.

Summary

As we analyzed the data to discover what factors contribute to the support of a music department, we found that faculty support is *not* related to winning contests but that student support and community support *are* reflected in the number of first division ratings recei ed in concert band contests. We cannot say whether this high support is the result of the director's winning first division ratings or the first division ratings are the result of strong community and student support. All we know is that the two go together and that the amount of community support and student support enjoyed by a director are dependent, to a real extent, upon his successful performance at concert band contests.

However, there are other factors even more highly correlated with faculty and community support. Their backing is greater when the high school is small and when it is the only high school in the district; when the director has been in the school for a long time; when the instrumental department was previously in poor condition; and when the director expresses cooperative attitudes toward the school administration and sees himself as a member of the total faculty, rather than as competing with them for student time and attention.

Those directors who win more concert band contests are more likely to report high community and student support. To promote support in the faculty, community, and student body, the band director must develop yet another set of skills. It helps if he is successful at public relations and promoting his department.

Chapter V

The Drop-Out Problem

The band director has a long-time personal investment in each of his bandsmen. This is especially true if he is in a small high school, starts his own beginners in elementary school, nurses them through junior high school, and counts on having them as stalwarts in his high school groups. It takes several years to develop a polished instrumentalist. Even those few directors who do have beginning programs for ninth graders cannot expect their late starters to become proficient enough on their instruments to occupy key positions in the high school band. When a high school bandsman drops out of the instrumental program, he cannot be replaced by someone else recruited from the high school's student body. If he happens to be a section leader — a key person in some section — this loss can be very damaging to the performance capabilities of the entire band.

To make the situation even more critical, a successful band program demands more student time, energy, and devotion than any other school activity except, perhaps, varsity athletics. With extra rehearsals, Saturday parades, and evening performances, a student cannot just be a casual bandsman. He frequently can stay in band only if he limits his participation in other activities. Choices and conflicts are inevitable.

Consequently, a major concern of every band director is that of keeping his bandsmen interested in band and keeping the drop-out rate at a minimum. Of course most teachers try to generate interest in their students, to motivate them to learn, and to keep them from dropping out of school. But the educational program of the academic teacher does not suffer if some students do choose to withdraw. This is not the case with the band or orchestra director. Any sizable student loss is immediately apparent in a decline in the quality of the band's performance. Consequently, band directors, more than other teachers, are preoccupied with motivating their students. They have devised almost every conceivable method for maintaining student interest.

Drop-Outs: Rates and Reasons

When we combine all the schools in the sample, the average high school instrumental program has 39 sophomores, 33 juniors, and 25 seniors in the total band program. This means that there is a 15% decline between the sophomore and junior year, and a 24% decline between the junior and senior year. There are no significant regional differences in the drop-out rate. If a band director starts with 100 sophomores and experiences an average drop-out rate, he will have 85 students from this sophomore class left in the junior year, and will graduate 65 bandsmen.

Each band director was asked the number of students he had lost from his band during the year in which he was interviewed and the reasons given by these students for withdrawing from band. Seventy-two per cent of the directors reported losing at least one student during the year because the family had moved out of town. Unfortunately, it appears that students who move out are never replaced by the number of students who move in. It may be that the continuity of band experience is broken when students change schools and many do not enroll in band at the new school.

Another reason for dropping band was the demand for time made by the band program. Sixty per cent of the directors reported losing students during the year because they could not stay in band and meet the requirements for college entrance; 20% had students drop because they were failing academic subjects and could not spare the time needed for band from their study time; and 44% reported that they had lost students because the students felt that band was taking too much time. Forty-six per cent of the directors reported that some students had dropped just because they got tired of band. Twenty-one per cent reported losing students because their parents wanted them to stop playing in band. The parental objections frequently centered on the time demands made by the band program. Evidently, rehearsals before and after school and in the evening take a serious toll.

Thirty-six per cent of the directors reported losing students because of class scheduling conflicts in the high school and 32% lost students because they wanted to play on varsity athletic teams and did not have time for both band and athletics. Relatively few losses were due to specific internal problems in the music program itself. Thirty-two per cent of the directors lost some students because they did not like to practice and another 14% lost students because the music was too difficult for them.

It takes time to prepare a large group for a performance, to coach soloists, and to work with ensembles — more time than is available during the school day. A bandsman must be willing to get out of bed earlier in order to make those before school rehearsals and he must give up having an after-school job or participating in athletics in order to come to after-school rehearsals. He must manage somehow to get his homework done before supper or in-between supper and the evening rehearsal. Considering these heavy demands, the average of 6.18 drop-outs per year is remarkably low. How do directors provide the kind of incentives needed to maintain this level of involvement for four years? What factors are most significant in reducing drop-outs?

Types of Motivations

Among the motivational techniques directors use to stimulate and sustain student interest in their departments are the following:

Group Incentives

Group-centered motivations are those rewards which flow from being a member of a recognized organization and sharing in the glory resulting from its victories in competition and its successful public performances. Such rewards for bandsmen come from participating in a band that is recognized for its excellence and its honors won in the competitive atmosphere of public school music. They may come also from participating in parades and concerts and in being part of an active organization — one which is well-regarded by the community, the faculty, and the student body as a whole.

If these group-centered rewards are important in motivating students to remain in band, then we would expect that bands which are recognized by university judges for their excellence; bands which are winning marching contests and are getting first division ratings in concert contests; bands which are supported by their communities, the high school staff, and the student body will have a lower drop-out rate than bands which do not provide this type of satisfaction.

The directors whose bands are getting first division ratings at concert band contests report significantly lower rates of drop-out.

There was no relationship between the *number* of parades and concerts in which the band participated and the drop-out rate. Maintaining a high level of activity, alone, is not enough to keep students interested. However, the level of support from groups outside the band was significant. Directors of bands with a low drop-out rate reported significantly more support from the faculty and from the community; they also reported more student support. Thus, the band director who wishes to minimize his drop-out rate — and this is essential to the maintenance of his organization — must strive to develop group incentives by winning concert contests and developing support for his organization in the school and community.

Individual Incentives

A second kind of reward comes from the honor and recognition which an individual student may receive for his own contribution to the organization. These are the individual incentives which each band director tries to build into his organization to motivate students to participate. Some directors have developed incentive systems which encourage students to practice by grading them according to the hours they practice, by giving special awards, or by seating them in their section according to the amount they practice. Some directors give important responsibilities to student officers in the band and identify them with chevrons, pins, bars, and other tokens of recognition (Sousa band award, etc.). Others use a challenge system in seating the concert band and make concert band seating a significant part of the reward structure. Still others use a point system in which individual students earn credit toward their band awards by accumulating points which are distributed according to their contribution to the group. If these individual incentives are important motivators, we would expect that band directors who make use of them would have lower drop-out rates than band directors who do not use them. This is exactly what we found.

Directors who identify their officers with chevrons, pins, braid, or officer bars, etc. have a significantly lower rate of drop-outs than those who have no officers or no rewards. Similarly, directors who choose a select group of bandsmen to act as a performing team for public performances have a lower drop-out rate than directors who use all their players for every public performance and have no system of selection. It does not matter whether the director uses a point system or a system of challenges to make selections. Interestingly enough, those directors who use a system of incentives which rewards "ranks" rather than individuals have a significantly higher drop-out rate than those who use individual rewards. Apparently, a critical factor in reducing drop-outs is to reward students individually and publicly for their contribution to the band and not to treat all students the same, irrespective of their contribution.

Many directors believe the overnight trip is an important factor in reducing drop-outs from their bands. They believe that one or two overnight trips a year in connection with some out-of-town performance provides a focus of anticipation and excitement for the entire year which serves as a motivation for students who otherwise might not continue with the organization. Statistical analysis proved this to be true! In general, those directors who have an overnight trip have a lower drop-out rate than directors who do not have an overnight trip during the year. Similarly, directors who report having a stage band also have significantly fewer drop-outs than those who do not have a stage band. Individual incentives and recognition, the pleasure of overnight excursions, and participating in a stage band all tend to motivate students to stay in band.

Interpersonal Rewards

A third type of reward is less tangible but may be a very important factor in reducing drop-outs — the relationship which develops between the director and his students. It is possible that the most important factor in reducing drop-outs is the director himself and how *he* feels about his students. Does a director who has a high opinion of his students' intelligence, who sees them as active and dynamic, who regards them as sociable and worthy, and who respects them as persons whose ideas should be considered in decision-making have fewer drop-outs than the director who has a low opinion of his students, maintains social distance between himself and his students, and does not involve them in decision-making?

When I examined these questions closely, I found that there is no correlation between drop-out rate and a director's involving students in decision-making, nor does it seem to matter whether a director tries to develop close, warm relations with students or remains somewhat distant. What *does* matter is how the director perceives his students when he rates their personality characteristics. Directors with a low drop-out rate perceive their students as significantly more intelligent and more cooperative than directors with high drop-out rates. Thus, the intangible quality of the interpersonal relationships between director and students is also a factor in drop-outs.

Summary

Drop-outs are a serious problem for every director. He has no recruiting activities or beginning band at the high school level. Consequently, his program inevitably suffers from gradual attrition which he can slow down but cannot completely stop. In general, his drop-out rate is lower if he has a band that is winning first division ratings at concert contests and has the support of the faculty and the community. Individual incentives, such as recognizing officers and others with special insignia and selecting only the most proficient players to perform in public are also associated with low drop-out rates. Having a stage band and going on overnight trips also reduce drop-outs. Finally, the attitude of the director toward his students is significant. Directors with the lowest percentage of drop-outs rated their students as more intelligent, more cooperative, and more helpful than directors with higher rates of attrition.

The relationship between low drop-out rate, high number of concert band contests won, and high community and staff support illustrates the pressures under which the typical band director operates.

Because he is expected to present polished public performances, he must maintain student involvement and minimize drop-outs. In order to achieve this, he develops an elaborate system of awards and incentives which tends to parallel that of the athletic department. He plans trips and out-of-town performances to keep his bandsmen interested and his program alive.

Chapter VI

Small School — Large School
New School — Old School

As I journeyed through the country, I found school after school exploding with students. Old buildings are surrounded by new additions; in some cases new buildings practically envelop the ancient structures. New schools are everywhere. Buildings range from conventional one-unit structures to the multiple-unit campus so common in California. Many of the new schools are beautiful, showing imagination and reflecting contemporary trends in architecture.

I found new high schools serving large, rural consolidated districts which were located in the open country, miles from any community. Students may be bussed to school from an area of over several hundred square miles. One such school in Indiana is named for a large, well-known city in Florida. Thinking that this was also the name of a town, I looked for the city on a map, without success. After asking directions, I drove for miles through farms and orchards, scarcely seeing a house. Finally, when I was positive that I must be completely lost, the school appeared in the middle of a huge field. No houses, no town, just a beautiful new school with many buses and an active band program.

The average of the high school buildings I visited was 22 years. Almost half have been established within the last 10 years. On the other hand, one school I visited was established 80 years ago, and there were 22 schools over 50 years of age. Interestingly enough, the age of the school is not related in any way to the quality of its music program. Older schools are no more likely to be nominated for outstanding bands than new schools. In fact, three of the nominated music departments are in large schools which had been in existence only a little more than a year when I visited them.

The Larger the High School, the Smaller the Percentage

The larger the high school, the larger the band but the smaller the percentage of students who take instrumental music. The average large high school in my sample had an enrollment of 1,993 students. The average small school had 699 students. This means that the average large high school had 2.8 times more students than the small high school. However, when we compare their instrumental programs, the large school has only 1.5 times more students in band. If the ratio were the same, the large high school, with its 2.8 times more students, would have an average of 249 band members.

We can look at the situation another way. The small high school band program, with an average of 89 students, includes 12.7% of the student body. The large high school band program, with an average of 133 participants, includes only 6.7% of the student body. Thus, we can draw two conclusions: (1) small schools are involving a larger percentage of their students in their instrumental programs, and (2) the size of the band will not increase in proportion to the size of the student body.

For 10 years I taught in a high school with a student population of 400. Our band averaged 80 members or 20% of the student body. I then moved to a large high school of 3,800 students. Over a period of several years, I have never been able to involve more than 200 bandsmen in the program, 5.3% of the student body. It would take 760 bandsmen to increase the instrumental program to 20% of that student body!

From these figures we can conclude that the student in a small high school has a greater probability of being involved in instrumental music than a student attending a large high school. This is definitely an advantage enjoyed by students enrolled in small high schools. Yet, even 12.7% is not a very impressive figure.

Most band directors in large high schools do not see the large student body as an opportunity to involve more students in their program but rather as an opportunity to apply more stringent screening procedures. In small schools, 72% of the directors permit all incoming bandsmen to enter the department without audition,but only 31% of the large high school instrumental departments operate without auditions. In 69% of the large high schools, all bandsmen are auditioned and students are placed in a band according to their level of musical capability. Most schools have a second band for less proficient players. There are a few directors who simply drop students who fail the audition but this occurs in less than 10% of the schools I visited.

The usual argument presented in favor of maintaining a second band and grouping according to ability is that it stimulates the more capable musicians and encourages them to expand their abilities to meet a higher level of performance. With the best players concentrated in one organization, the director can select more difficult music, can extend his emphasis on sight reading, and give greater polish to the numbers being performed. It is argued that the slower student, placed in an organization playing music which is technically too difficult for him, becomes discouraged and drops out.

Where there is no ability grouping, as in most small high schools, the director must select music to accommodate a wide variation in musical skill. He must compromise by selecting music which may be too simple to challenge his best players. This also creates a problem. The better student, not fully challenged by the music, may lose interest, especially in his senior year.

However, less skillful musicians learn a great deal from the more advanced players. Upperclassmen can be used as section leaders and tutors to assist the younger bandsmen. Less proficient players sitting next to a fine musician can observe correct technique and hear better interpretation, tone quality, and intonation. If students of varying advancement are segregated, there is less opportunity for this informal, pupil-to-pupil teaching and learning. This type of teaching is also being encouraged in academic classes today. From data in this study, we cannot say which procedure produces the most proficient performing groups.

Departments using ability grouping did not receive any more nominations by the university judges than schools with outstanding departments using heterogeneous grouping. Thus, the issue of heterogeneous versus homogeneous grouping is still unresolved in instrumental music education just as it is unanswered in general education.

The Trend Toward Larger High Schools

In the early part of this century, at the crest of the adult community band movement which established the pattern for instrumental music in the public schools, most high schools had less than 1,000 students. Thousands of high schools in rural communities had fewer than 500 students and many had fewer than 100 students. The performance-oriented competitive aspects of public school music flourished in such an atmosphere. Civic pride was fostered by the local high school and its band.

However, the small rural high school in which performance-oriented competitive music flourished is gradually disappearing. When compiling the ballots for the study, I compared the number of large high schools (student body of 1,000 or more) with the number of small high schools (student body of 400-999) in each state. The three most rural states, Iowa, Kansas, and Texas, had 6.6, 4.3, and 2.1 small high schools to every large high school, respectively. Other rural states had ratios between 1.2 and 2.0. The five most rapidly growing urban states, New York, California, Florida, Illinois, and Washington, had a ratio of 5.5, 3.2, 1.6, 1.2, and 1.2 large high schools for every small high school, respectively.

51

The number of small high schools is gradually dwindling as a result of rural school consolidation. For example, in 1930, there were 4,399,000 pupils enrolled in 23,930 public secondary schools (including junior high schools). In 1966 there were 11,700,000 pupils enrolled in 26,700 secondary schools. The number of students increased 168% but the number of secondary schools increased only 11% during the 36 intervening years. The average number of students per high school has more than doubled in that period (United States Census, 1960.) The trend is for more and more students to be educated in fewer but larger high schools.

High schools with over one thousand students are clearly the wave of the future. Therefore, comparisons between the instrumental programs in small high schools today and large high schools today will reveal, to some extent, what the future holds for instrumental music.

Equal Number of Performances

The number of performances given by a band neither increases nor decreases with high school enrollment; 50% of the large high schools compete in marching band contests and 50% of the small schools, while 76% of the large schools compete in concert band contests and 81% of the small schools. An average of 21 musicians participate in solo contests from each large high school compared to 20 musicians from small schools. The large school averages 13 ensembles each year compared to 12 ensembles for small schools.

The pace of out-of-school rehearsals is comparable. During marching season, the average large high school director holds 1.97 extra rehearsals per week while the average small high school band director holds 1.94. In concert season the averages are 1.42 and 2.67, respectively. The average large high school band presents slightly more halftime shows (6.5) than the small high school (6.0), but participates in the same number of parades, about 3.5. The large high school also presents a slightly larger number of concerts, 5.5 per year compared to 4.7 for small high schools. Although the dynamics of the value system which fosters a performance-oriented instrumental program were first generated in a society of small high schools, they continue, with equal force, in the large high schools of today.

Quality of the Music Program

The typical instrumental teacher in the large high school teaches three classes of instrumental music a day in high school while the typical instrumental teacher in the small high school teaches only two high school instrumental classes a day, spending the extra time in elementary schools. This does not necessarily mean students in large high schools get more individual attention. When we think in terms of teaching hours per student, the small high school director spends two periods a day with 89 students or an average of 44 pupils per hour while the large high school director spends three hours with 133 students and also teaches an average of 44 students per hour. From this perspective, there is little difference in the amount of attention which a student receives.

The large high school receives an average of 61 new bandsmen each year from junior high while small high schools can expect an average of 35. The average large high school receives students from 2.6 junior high schools while small high schools receive students from an average of 1.4 junior high schools. Thus, the large high school receives 23 students yearly from each of its junior high schools while the small high school receives about 25 students per junior high school. The size of the program in junior high school, therefore, is very similar and the chief difference in the total number of students at the high school level is determined by the number of junior high schools feeding bandsmen into the high school.

During the marching season the large high school uses an average of 95 bandsmen in its marching band compared to 78 for the small high school. This is an average difference of 17 players. Then an interesting phenomenon occurs during concert season. The average large high school reports having a concert band of 80 players which is *two less* than the 82 players reported by the small high school! Of course, this is readily explained. As was noted earlier, the large high school frequently has an intermediate band designed for the less proficient bandsmen. These young people are assigned to this second band as soon as they are no longer needed for marching performances. On the other hand, the small high school director must use every player available for both marching and concert bands in order to maintain a complete instrumentation.

Individual lessons and ensembles are another way in which we can assess the amount of individual attention a student receives. The typical large school director is giving lessons to 21 students while the small school director is working with 29 students individually. Seventy-three per cent of the large high school directors did not give any lessons at all compared with 51% of the small school directors. Thus, an instrumental student is more likely to receive individual lessons in a small high school.

Both large and small high school directors work with an equal number of ensembles. Since there are more students in large high school programs, this actually means that a smaller percentage of bandsmen in the large high school bands is involved in playing in ensembles.

We must conclude that, in general, the bandsman in the large high school gets slightly less individual attention than the bandsman in the small high school even though the director spends an average of one period a day more teaching instrumental music. It is probable that many bandsmen from large high schools receive outside-of-school private lessons.

Breadth of Music Education

Except for the fact that 75% of the large high schools and only 20% of the small high schools have an intermediate band, there is little difference between the two in the variety of band organizations availble for student participation. All schools, regardless of size, have pep bands, used for basketball games and pep rallies. Sixty-five per cent of both the large and small schools have a stage band. Almost none of the high schools I visited have a beginning band program at the high school level. Those which do have beginning band are almost exclusively a few large high schools.

In one respect, however, the large high school provides more opportunity for music education than the small high school. It offers a wider variety of music courses beyond the band program. Eighty per cent of the large high schools have an orchestra, while only 20% of the small high schools have orchestras. Regional differences are very marked: 79% of the Pacific coast schools visited had an orchestra; 61% of the Great Lakes schools; 56% of the Midwestern schools; but only 33% of the Southern schools. To some extent, these regional differences reflect differences in the size of the high schools in the sample. The Pacific coast has more large high schools than any other region.

There are several reasons why orchestras do not flourish in small high schools. In the small school there is always a shortage of students to participate in school programs. The most able students are recruited by other departments — the athletic coaches, the drama coach, the debating team, the school paper, the yearbook, and the music department, which includes both instrumental and vocal groups. There is a limit to the number of activities in which even the best student can participate. Consequently, he has to make a choice.

Sometimes students or parents may prefer the band to the orchestra. Several years ago, I accepted a position teaching in a small town of about 10,000 persons. There was no orchestra, but there had been a successful band program. Upon arriving at the school, I discovered that the district owned 24 violins, several violas, cellos, and string basses. I began immediately to develop plans to organize both a band and an orchestra. During the recruiting period, my enthusiasm was sufficiently contagious to generate student interest in playing strings and all of the string instruments were issued to beginners within a week. Much to my disappointment, by the end of the following week, most of the string instruments had been returned by *parents* who did not want their children playing strings. They wanted them to play band instruments. They were more familiar with the band and did not want to suffer through the initial pangs of learning a string instrument.

Finances are also a major consideration in the small school. There is often insufficient money to support both band and orchestra. Most schools have an active athletic program and expect a band to perform at football games, basketball games, and other athletic events. Some of the expense of equipping the band may be met if the athletic department contributes a certain percentage of the gate receipts to the band's operating fund. The band is also able to provide music for many community events such as parades and patriotic programs. Consequently, if there can be only a single organization, it is usually the band which is chosen.

In many cases, it is primarily a matter of limited time. The band director in the small high school is often in charge of instrumental music for the entire school system. He starts the beginners in the elementary grades, directs the elementary and junior high school bands, and gives lessons in addition to directing the high school band. He may even be the choir director. Under these circumstances, there is not enough time for one director to also develop a string program for an orchestra.

Large high schools are also significantly more likely to offer music courses other than performing groups. Sixty per cent of the large high schools have theory classes compared to only 18% of the small schools; 34% offer music history and appreciation compared to 10% of the small schools; 5% of the large schools have piano classes. As high schools increase in size, we can anticipate a wider variety of music offerings and increased attention to preparing students to be consumers of music. This tendency in the large high schools, however, is minimal and should not obscure the fact that the majority of all high school music departments do not offer such courses and have strictly performance-oriented programs.

The Nature of the Band Director's Job

The work assignment of instrumental teachers in larger high schools is quite different from that in small high schools. Regardless of the size of the school, most band directors teach only instrumental music — only 30% are assigned also to teach one or more academic subjects. However, as high schools become larger, we can anticipate more music teachers with more specialization within the field of instrumental music, including elementary instrumental teaching as differentiated from high school teaching.

Most instrumental music teachers in small high schools have a teaching assignment which includes the elementary school program. Directors in the large schools frequently teach only in the high school, and the responsibility for the elementary school program is delegated to other staff members. The small high school director spends an average of 2.5 periods a day teaching instrumental classes in the elementary school while the average large high school director spends less than one period a day in elementary teaching. Seventy per cent of them do not teach any elementary classes at all. By contrast, only 23% of the teachers in small high schools have no responsibility whatsoever for elementary school programs.

Some directors assume the role of supervisor for the elementary program. In my sample, 17% of the large school directors were serving as elementary music supervisors, but did no elementary teaching. This was also true for 19% of the small high school directors. Fifty-nine per cent of the directors in the large schools said they had no responsibility of any kind in the elementary school. The same percentage (59%) of the directors in small high schools reported that they did *all* the teaching of instrumental music at all levels: elementary, junior and senior high school. These differences are statistically significant and nationwide.

Finally, when I asked band directors to rate their satisfaction with their jobs, 78% of the small school directors reported that they were *very* satisfied with their jobs compared with 65% of the directors teaching in large schools. This is true even though the large school directors were paid an average salary of $10,674 while the average salary of the small school director was $9,052.

One School — One Band Director

Just as a school needs one yearbook and one newspaper, regardless of its size, in a performance-oriented tradition, a school needs only one band. The national pattern is one school — one band — one band director, regardless of the size of the student body. In my survey, 65% of the high schools with over a thousand students had one band director and 64% of those with less than a thousand students also had one band instructor. Only 35% of the band directors in my sample had other instrumental teachers working with them. Twenty-five per cent had one additional person and the other 10% had three or more colleagues.

The number of colleagues had no relationship, whatsoever, to the size of the school. However, those schools having more than one instrumental teacher were significantly more likely to be nominated by university judges as having outstanding departments. Sixty-six

56

per cent of the nominated schools had more than one person in the high school instrumental department, while only 25% of the matched schools had that many teachers.

When schools grow in size, the number of staff members in every department of the school enlarges proportionately — *except for music teachers.* Large high schools have more social studies teachers, more coaches, more homemaking teachers, more science teachers, even more counselors and vice-principals than small high schools, *but they do not have significantly more music teachers!* In this study, the average small high school has 1.4 instrumental teachers and the average large high school has 1.6.

Summary

As rural schools consolidate and more families move to urban areas, the size of individual high schools is not expanding proportionately. This pattern has serious implications for music education as a profession. It means that music education in the future will be even more elitist than in the past because a smaller percentage of students in large high schools participate in performing groups. Students will receive less individual attention (in school) but there will be a greater variety of musical course offerings. There will probably be more homogeneous grouping in the music education of the future and more differentiation between elementary and secondary teaching with fewer band directors teaching at more than one level.

Even more significant for the profession, the "one school — one band director" tradition based on the performance-oriented role of music education in the past places a strict ceiling on the total number of music educators who will be needed. While the number of teachers in other subject areas increases in proportion to the increase in the number of students in the school, this is not true of music teachers. As long as we are music makers serving an elite group rather than music educators who touch all or most students, the pattern will remain approximately one band director, one vocal director, perhaps one orchestra director per school — regardless of the number of students in the school.

Chapter VII

The "Metropolitan Lid"

Urbanization means more than just larger high schools; it also means more high schools per school district. The typical small or medium-sized town has one high school which serves the entire community. All community loyalties are centered in a single school which is frequently a focus for local pride because of its outstanding athletic teams or music groups. Communities actively vie with each other. Interest and support run high.

What happens when the small community grows and the second, third, fourth, or fifth high school is added? This is the typical situation in most urban school districts and is even more extreme in the large metropolitan school districts. For example, at the time of my study, Chicago had 61 high schools, Los Angeles had 54, and Dallas had 21.

In order to gain some insight into the future of instrumental music as we move into the era of the urban district, I will examine the influence of the multiple high school district on instrumental music programs.

Since each university judge received ballots which contained the names of all the high schools in his state with an enrollment of more than 400 students, and each judge was asked to rank, in order, the 10 large high schools with the most outstanding instrumental departments and the 10 small high schools, the results show that very few high schools were nominated from large metropolitan school districts such as Chicago and Los Angeles. Why? Could there be a "metropolitan lid" which operates to keep metropolitan schools from developing outstanding performing groups? I decided to pursue this question further by analyzing the distribution of large high schools nominated by the judges according to the type of school district in which they are located. I classified all large high schools appearing on the ballots sent to university judges into four groups.

1. *Metropolitan high schools* are those located in cities with a population of 250,000 or more. These are schools in large districts containing many high schools.

2. *Suburban high schools* are those located within 75 miles of a population center of 250,000 which are not part of the metropolitan school district.

3. *Middle city high schools* are located in communities of between 150,000 and 250,000 persons which are more than 75 miles from any metropolitan center.

4. *Regional town high schools* are those located in communities more than 75 miles away from a metropolitan area that have a population of under 150,000. Many such schools are in small rural towns and in districts which have only one or two high schools.

The large school ballots mailed to college directors contained 220 metropolitan high schools, 581 suburban high schools, 25 middle city high schools, and 201 regional town high schools. The bar chart in Figure 5 compares the percentage of schools nominated in each category with the percentage in that category.

The 220 metropolitan high schools on the ballots were 21% of all the large schools in the states studied. Therefore, we would expect that 21% of all the nominated large high schools would be metropolitan schools, if they were selected in proportion to their percentage on the ballots. Instead, metropolitan schools were underchosen. The judges selected only 12 metropolitan high schools, 11% of the total schools nominated and only half as many as would be expected on the basis of their proportion of the total list.

On the other hand, there were 201 regional towns listed on the ballot, 19% of all the large high schools in the states visited. We would expect 19% of the nominated large schools to be from regional towns but, instead, 40 regional town schools were selected, 35% of those nominated. This is 17 more towns than we would have expected had they been selected in proportion. High schools of over 1,000 pupils from regional towns have over three times as many good bands than those from metropolitan centers.

Multiple High School Districts

Because of the significance of this finding, I made a second independent test for the presence of the "metropolitan lid." If there is a "metropolitan lid"which depresses the quality of performing groups in school districts with numerous high schools, then one would expect to find significantly more non-nominated large schools coming from districts with many high schools and more nominated large schools coming from districts with fewer high schools.

This is exactly what was found. Sixty-six per cent of the large nominated schools were located in districts having only one or two high schools. On the other hand, only 48% of the large schools which were

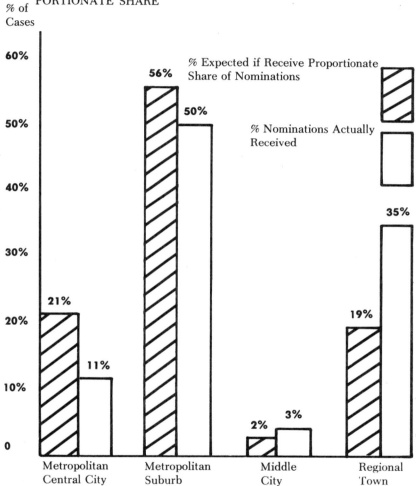

Figure 5

NATIONAL COMPARISON OF PERCENTAGES OF NOMINA—
TIONS RECEIVED BY FOUR TYPES OF HIGH SCHOOLS
(WITH 1,000 - STUDENTS EACH) WITH THE PERCENTAGE
WHICH WOULD BE EXPECTED IF EACH RECEIVED ITS PRO—
PORTIONATE SHARE

% of
Cases

% Expected if Receive Proportionate
Share of Nominations

% Nominations Actually
Received

56%
50%
35%
21%
11%
19%
2%
3%

Metropolitan
Central City

Metropolitan
Suburb

Middle
City

Regional
Town

(a) Differences of this magnitude would occur by chance less than
time in ten thousand (Chi Square=24.6 p<.001)

This chart is based upon a total of 220 Metropolitan City Schools,
581 Metropolitan Suburb Schools, 25 Middle City Schools, and 201
Regional Town Schools

Recommended schools by college band directors

not mentioned appeared in districts with one or two high schools.

Put another way, the non-nominated schools were located in districts with an average of 4.2 high schools, while the nominated schools had only an average of 2.7 high schools in their districts. High schools in multiple high school districts are significantly less likely to be chosen by university judges. There is a "metropolitan lid" on outstanding performing groups.

What Produces the "Metropolitan Lid?"

Many of the factors which I thought might account for the "metropolitan lid" did not prove to be significant. There is no difference in either the age or the job satisfaction of directors in the two types of schools. The metropolitan directors reported an average salary for the academic year of $9,706 compared to $9,594 paid to directors in districts with fewer high schools. These differences are so small that they could easily have happened by chance.

Concert and marching band schedules are much the same in both groups, but there is one respect in which metropolitan directors have a *slight* advantage over directors in districts with fewer high schools. Thirty-one per cent of the metropolitan bands are receiving physical education credit for band, compared to 19% of the schools in the smaller districts. A larger number of bands in metropolitan high schools meet for two hours during the regular school day instead of one hour.

The metropolitan director reports an average of 122 instrumentalists compared to an average of 136 bandsmen in the schools in smaller districts, a difference that is not large enough to be statistically significant. Both types of directors report approximately the same number of auxiliary units such as flag and baton twirlers, color guards, and drill teams. Both types of bands participate in about the same number of activities in the course of a year. What makes the difference?

Each director was asked the number of subjects other than instrumental music which he teaches daily. I found that the metropolitan director is expected to teach significantly more non-instrumental classes each day. The directors in large multi-high school districts average 1.3 non-instrumental classes a day compared to .4 non-instrumental classes for directors in districts with only one or two high schools. These differences are significant. Thus, one of the major differences between multi-high school district schools and those located in smaller districts is that directors in the former are required to spend more of their time teaching and preparing for classes in non-instrumental subjects and have less time to concentrate on the instrumental program.

There is also a significant difference in the amount of money beyond the school budget which is available to instrumental departments in

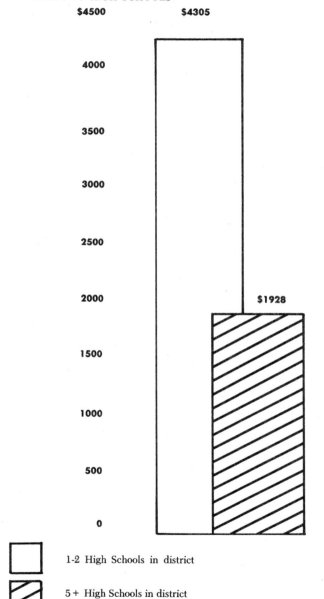

Figure 6

COMPARISON OF THE AVERAGE YEARLY BAND BUDGET
FOR HIGH SCHOOLS IN DISTRICTS WITH FIVE OR MORE HIGH
SCHOOLS TO THAT OF HIGH SCHOOLS IN DISTRICTS WITH
ONE OR TWO HIGH SCHOOLS

1-2 High Schools in district

5 + High Schools in district

the two kinds of districts. Metropolitan high schools spend an average of $1,928 a year beyond the school budget on the music program compared to $4,305 being spent annually by the high schools in smaller districts. Figure 6 presents a dramatic picture of this difference.

A more detailed look at spending patterns reveals that metropolitan schools are spending an average of $836 a year on new equipment compared to $1,622 being spent by the large schools in small districts. They spend an average of only $474 a year on music compared to $770 spent by schools in smaller districts.

In addition, the metropolitan directors reported receiving significantly less community and faculty support: the larger the number of high schools, the lower the faculty and community support scores. No differences were found in student support.

To summarize, high schools of 1,000 or more students in multiple high school districts are less likely to be nominated by university judges for their outstanding programs. The director is expected to teach more non-instrumental classes, has less money beyond the school budget on which to operate his department, and enjoys less faculty and community support.

Impact of the "Metropolitan Lid" on Instrumental Programs

Although the personal experiences of individual band directors who are teaching in multi-high school districts cannot be used to establish statistical trends, they do provide valuable insights into what happens to a performance-oriented instrumental music program in a large educational bureaucracy. In this section, my own experience and the experiences of other directors will be used to illustrate how the "metropolitan lid" operates.

One director I interviewed is teaching in a district containing eight high schools. As the district has grown, his central administration has faced pressing financial problems. At one time, the bands in his district were active in parades, and contests, but the expense of providing school busses for such events finally became so heavy that the board of trustees developed a policy prohibiting bands from participating in out-of-town events. When problems occur in one high school, the district is prone to develop a policy that affects all the high schools in an attempt to eliminate any controversy. For example, friction developed between the flag and baton twirlers attached to the band in one high school so the district now has a policy of no twirlers. One of the band booster clubs became overly active and created some problems in one high school so the board decided to prohibit booster clubs. A girl drum major in one school was criticized for her costume;

subsequently, the board ruled that all girl drum majors must wear long trousers and a coat. Once such policies are established, they are almost impossible to change.

In another multiple high school district, there is a precise formula which determines the number of instruments the school board will provide for any school. This formula is related to the size of the student body not the size of the band. If an ambitious director recruits a larger number of interested musicians than can be equipped using this formula and cannot provide instruments with the money allotted, he is responsible for securing the extra finances needed for additional instruments himself. No adjustment is made in the formula for schools offering both band and orchestra, so the temptation is to use the available finances to develop only one good organization.

Another large district provides a central warehouse for storing instruments which are not in use. If needed, they are available to other high schools. In the abstract, this sounds like a good principle. However, no director wants to relinquish his surplus instruments for fear the time will come when he will need them and the central warehouse will have them checked out to some other high school. Consequently, there are just no "surplus" instruments available.

Another district regulates the number of band members who can be used in pep bands. Directors are allowed 15 persons in the football pep band, but only 10 in the basketball pep band. The director has no discretion in this matter.

Another director was in the middle of a controversy over band uniforms at the time I visited him. One of the board members had suggested that the district save money by purchasing the same basic uniform for all the high schools in the system. This would permit high schools to exchange uniforms and the district could get a much better discount because it would be buying uniforms in larger quantities. An individual director would have no control over the uniform for his band.

One metropolitan high school had a young director in his middle 20's. He had accepted the position because the instrumental department was weak and he liked the challenge this situation presented. With hard work and enthusiasm, the band and orchestra were soon flourishing under his leadership. They performed for numerous school assemblies and were well-received. Encouraged by this success, he felt that the time had come for his groups to perform for other audiences. He spoke to his principal about organizing an exchange concert with one of the other high schools in the district. The principal was quite agreeable, but such a request had to be channeled through the superintendent's office. When the request went to a higher level, it was denied. The young director was informed that such an exchange concert might encourage more such exchanges and the district could not afford to furnish bus transportation. In addition, such exchanges might promote invidious comparisons. If one high school has a flourishing program, this might cast a shadow on the other high schools in the district with less adequate programs. The superintendent did not like the possibility of competition among district high schools. The young director was planning to resign at the end of the school year.

Another director is teaching in a high school located directly in the center of a large metropolis. A man in his middle 50's, he has chosen to teach in a slum area where youngsters are in constant turmoil because he believes this kind of teaching is more meaningful. The average income for families of children attending this high school was under $3,000 a year. The school has expanded and temporary buildings have been erected on the football field, leaving the band no field for rehearsal. Although he starts 50 beginners each year, he ends the year with only a few. However, the drop-out problem is not nearly as serious as the police problem. Just about the time a section in his band is complete and begins to improve, one or two bandsmen disappear to juvenile hall or youth training schools. Just keeping a viable organization is a major problem.

It wasn't until I returned from interviewing and had seen the "metropolitan lid" operating in other districts, that I realized that a "metropolitan lid" was closing in on my own district. I feel like a medical doctor who is able to diagnose his own illness, recognize that it may be terminal, but is unable to do much about it.

When I accepted a position in my present district, there were only two high schools. One of these schools had been open for only four years. The following year, the school board opened a third high school, and three years later, it opened a fourth high school. A fifth school was opened within another three years.

During the time when the district had only two high schools, my department grew from 30 bandsmen to over 200. The budget increased from a few dollars a year to between eight and ten thousand dollars annually. However, as the number of high schools increased, the central administration was pressed for funds to finance an ever-expanding student population. A music budget which originally financed programs in two high schools now had to support four and then five high schools. Restrictions on new equipment were tightened, music budgets were decreased, and all schools were placed on a strict budget.

As the district expanded, other restrictions were enforced. Rules were passed to limit participation in out-of-town events because bus transportation for so many groups was too expensive. The overnight trip, which had been the highlight of each year's activity, was gradually abolished when the district found itself furnishing bus transportation for four and then five active high school bands. Initially, the board established a rotation system which allowed two bands to have an overnighter each year. This was still too expensive. As pressures and financial obligations increased, the overnight trip became an ever-greater burden and was eventually abolished.

As each new school was organized, it received band members from older high schools which had formerly served its residential area. New directors faced the problem of developing loyalty to the new school and weaning band members away from former attachments. Competitive feelings emerged between the students in the music groups of the various high schools. On one occasion, the bands in the district were asked to present a combined halftime performance for the All Star Pro-Bowl game. This invitation offered an opportunity for the five high school bands to work together in a non-competitive project which would include all the students in each instrumental department. After some resistance, all five directors agreed to participate, selected a theme, and worked out a rehearsal schedule. However, band members had developed competitive feelings toward other bands in the district and the directors were startled to discover that their students did not share their own enthusiasm for the joint halftime show. Members of the parent booster clubs reacted negatively. Drill team sponsors were reluctant to pool their efforts. The principals of the five high schools were skeptical about the joint rehearsal plan. Initial rehearsals found members from different high schools taunting each other with derogatory remarks. In spite of these obstacles, the directors persisted. The final performance reflected a spirit of cooperation but the obstacles had been numerous. The "metropolitan lid" is hard to combat.

On the other hand, there were two metropolitan high schools which I visited that were ranked very high by the college nominators. The characteristics of these schools provide some insight into the kind of school which is able to maintain a performance-oriented program in the metropolitan school district.

One of these schools is located in a section of the city occupied by white collar and professional families. Eight years ago, the director helped open this school. Receiving students from 13 junior high schools, he has built a department which now boasts three concert bands plus a fourth band which trains new students. Each of the three concert bands has received first division ratings from the time the school first opened. Forty per cent of the bandsmen take private lessons from two symphony men who come to the high school for that purpose. These lessons are paid for from tax funds.

All freshmen are assigned to a freshman band, and sophomores are assigned to a sophomore band. However, junior and senior bandsmen are grouped together. During marching season, the schedule is arranged so that all bandsmen are able to have two periods of band a day.

His budget is ample. It allows him to buy recording basses, contrabass clarinets, and other desirable but expensive instruments. All money allocated to this high school is channeled through the principal and distributed to various departments as he sees fit. *The principal is a former band director!*

The other very successful instrumental program was in a metropolitan technical high school which has very high standards for admission, and has many more applicants than it can accept. Multiple annexes have made the football field a thing of the past. When I arrived for the interview, the director was conversing with a student and parent. He later explained that this type of interview is a regular procedure. Admission to the high school band is based on two types of evaluation: academic excellence and an interview. Young people applying for admission to the instrumental program are college preparatory students who have already decided on their area of interest. Aspiring music students are carefully screened and must pass an extensive audition before being accepted. Many students pay tuition to attend this high school because they live outside the city limits and are not eligible by reason of residence.

The three departmental bands, consisting of over 250 musicians, each play a full concert once a month. Members of ensembles are selected by audition and give formal concerts for the public. Sectional rehearsals are scheduled for 7:00 a.m. Once a week each section meets with the director during this hour while two additional days a week are spent in sectional rehearsals with a student leader. Emphasis is also placed on theory classes, sight singing, melodic dictation, and music history. The department has six instrumental teachers.

Summary

Our analysis of instrumental music programs in metropolitan school districts has shown that there is a "metropolitan lid" which appears to limit performance-oriented programs in large metropolitan districts.

Some factors which may account for these differences are that directors in metropolitan districts are teaching more non-instrumental classes, have less money to work with, and enjoy less staff and community support. The two most successful metropolitan instrumental departments in the states studied were special cases built on elitist principles. One school was located in an affluent neighborhood; the other had great prestige and a policy of restricted admissions.

Unfortunately, I did not ask questions during the interview which would deal directly with the "metropolitan lid" because I did not recognize its existence until I began analyzing the data from the interviews. Consequently, the present study offers only a glimpse of a phenomenon which could be very significant to the future of performance-oriented music education. This much we do know. As the number of high schools in a district increases, there is a lid which gradually settles on the instrumental program. This "metropolitan lid" seems to demand conformity and discourage innovation.

Suburbs of metropolitan centers often appear to avoid the "metropolitan lid" and frequently have outstanding school bands and orchestras.

Chapter VIII

The Profile of a "Successful" Director

During the course of each interview, every director answered many questions about himself, his education, and his feelings about being a band director. The similarity in the background and experiences of the directors in the sample is very remarkable. With this information, we can sketch a profile of the American band director which will describe quite accurately most of the men who were visited.

American band directors (86% in this study) played in high school bands and 41% decided to become band directors because of their music experiences in high school and their contact with their high school band directors. Eight had fathers who were band directors. Most (60%) went to universities or colleges with an enrollment of over 5,000 students. Almost all of the colleges (92%) offered music as a program for study and practically every band director (85%) enrolled as a music major with the intention of preparing to teach instrumental music in the public schools. Only 17 directors originally majored in some field other than music and then later decided to become an instrumental teacher. Another four were converts from vocal music and five began with the intention of playing their instruments professionally and then later decided to go into teaching. While in college, 80% played and marched in the college marching band, and 59% played and marched for four or more years. Even more, 94%, played in concert band in college, and 81% played for four or more years.

In retrospect, 39% of the directors felt that the most valuable work they had taken in college was either their course in instrumental methods or their lessons on their major and minor instruments. Another 7% thought that participating in marching band had been the most valuable experience. Music literature, music history, and theory, taken together, were mentioned by only 14% of the directors, and orchestra was not mentioned at all. When asked to evaluate their music education in college and name the area in which they felt their preparation had been most deficient, the emphasis again was on skills needed for music performances — 18% wished they had been given more training in marching band techniques and band organization; 16% would like to have had more training in instrument methods; and 6% wished they had received broader exposure to band literature.

Only one director reported that he did not have a major instrument. Three wind instruments accounted for well over half of the instrumental majors: 28% majored on trumpet; 27% on clarinet; and 16% on trombone. There were only four string majors who ended up directing a band. About 80% of the directors still play their major instrument and over half of them use this instrument in teaching.

The average band director is 41 years old, has been teaching for 16 years, and has taught in only two or three districts including the one in which he is now teaching. Seventy per cent began teaching in a high school with fewer than 1,000 students and 43% began teaching in a high school with fewer than 400 students. About 30% taught vocal as well as instrumental music on their first job, but only 15% have taught academic subjects. Even fewer have taught theory (2%) or music appreciation (8%). Their teaching and their education have been highly specialized from the very beginning and they continue to focus almost exclusively on instrumental music (bands).

At the time I visited with them, 78% of the band directors had earned an M.A. degree and an additional 14% were working on a master's degree. Almost all band directors are married (94%), only 12 were bachelors and just one divorced. An interesting sidelight — most band directors are Protestant (86%).

The picture which emerges is very consistent. The typical American band director decided to become a band director while still in high school because of the influence of his high school director. He entered college with the specific intention of becoming a band director, and participated in both marching and concert band throughout his college career. He entered teaching as a band director and has not been asked to teach anything else but band. In his opinion, the best courses he took in college were those which taught him how to be a band director, and he is most critical of those areas in his education which he believes have not helped him as an instrumental teacher and a performance technician. Significantly, 69% are "very satisfied" to be teaching band and 84% want to be teaching band five years from now either in their present position or in a college position.

Factors Irrelevant To "Success"

What distinguishes a man who is regarded by others as an outstanding band director? Is it his educational background? His instrumental techniques? His teaching methods? His educational philosophy? Who succeeds in our performance-oriented system? Who does not succeed?

One of the most significant findings of this study is that few of those characteristics of a director which seem to be logically related to success proved to be relevant while other characteristics not even considered before the data analysis proved to be very relevant indeed. Certain characteristics are common to all band directors in the sample. For example, all band directors have a bachelor's degree and most of them have a master's degree. Almost all directors were music majors, specialized in public school music, and played in high school and college bands. Therefore, these characteristics and others like them cannot be used as characteristics to distinguish successful from unsuccessful directors. We must look to those characteristics on which band directors differ to find what leads to success.

Educational Background

Although most directors have a master's degree, they attended schools of various sizes and prestige. Some did their undergraduate work in schools with less than one thousand students. However, size of school is not related to success. The man from the small college is just as likely to be nominated as an outstanding director as the man from a large university. Some directors went to teachers' colleges, others attended private religious colleges, a few went to music conservatories, some went to minor state colleges, and many attended large public universities. Some directors did their undergraduate work at colleges giving only the bachelor's degree, many went to colleges giving the master's degree, and about a fourth attended universities granting the doctorate. It made no difference in their ultimate success.

A director's choice of graduate school is just as inconsequential to his success as his choice of undergraduate school. Men with master's degrees from small private colleges fared as well as men with degrees from large state universities.

Although most band directors participated in marching and concert band in college, the few who did not were just as successful as those who did. There were 15 directors who played in college concert bands for a year or less — seven were nominated and eight were not nominated. Where a man goes to get his education and the amount of his college experience in performing groups is irrelevant to his eventual success as a band director in the public schools.

Techniques and Methods

The questionnaire is filled with questions inquiring about the techniques and methods which directors use in working with their groups. I had expected to find a set of techniques used by successful directors which could be shared with other band directors. Surely, the information gleaned from the years of experience in instrumental music of the 197 directors in the matched sample would yield certain organizational methods, musical skills, and technical knowledge that would differentiate the successful directors from the less successful.

What about the number of students receiving individual instrumental lessons as part of the school program? Surely, students in outstanding bands must get more individual attention than students in less notable organizations. Sixty-six per cent of the nominated schools and 73% of the matched schools give no lessons. The difference is not statistically significant. There were questions about the method used for scheduling private lessons. Does the successful director use a rotation system? Study hall periods? Before school? After school? Take students out of physical education? It does not matter. Most directors do not give individual lessons and those who do are no more likely to have outstanding bands than those who do not.

Perhaps successful directors make more use of sectional rehearsals. True, there are more directors who hold sectional rehearsals than directors who give private lessons, but the percentage is about the same for the nominated directors (38%) as for the non-nominated (36%).

What about private lessons? Perhaps outstanding bands have more students receiving individual instruction from private teachers and this is the key to their success. *Here there was a difference.* The average nominated band had 29.5 students taking private lessons and the average matched band had 21.7, a statistically small but significant difference.

What about incentives to practice? Could it be that successful directors have discovered some powerful motivational device unknown to the rest of us? Fifty-two per cent of them use no incentives at all compared to 62% of the non-nominated directors. This is not a very statistically significant difference.

How about schools with orchestras? Having an orchestra provides an additional opportunity for the better wind students to play symphonic works, sharpen their finesse, and develop their playing techniques. It seems a reasonable hypothesis; but orchestra, too, is irrelevant to success. Sixty per cent of the nominated bands and 62% of the non-nominated bands were in schools also offering orchestra. Piano classes, theory classes, music history and appreciation classes are also irrelevant. Bands from schools with these broader offerings are no more likely to be outstanding than those from schools offering only band.

Almost every school has some kind of summer instrumental program; consequently, the summer music program, *per se*, cannot make the difference. However, it could be that more students participate in summer music camps from the outstanding departments. Although the nominated directors report an average of 15 of their students attending summer camp compared to an average of 11 for non-nominated directors, this difference could be due to chance.

Some directors believe that having a stage band will give additional verve to their instrumental program and will broaden the musical experience of the students who participate. However, this hypothesis must also fall: 65% of the nominated and 72% of the non-nominated schools have stage bands.

Some directors are strong believers in the challenge system and the point system. They believe both techniques stimulate practice, foster competition among bandsmen, and improve the quality of performance. Is this a factor? Most directors use a challenge system: 70% of the nominated and 67% of the non-nominated bands use some form of public or private challenge. However, the method did not distinguish successful from less successful bands.

Only a few directors (30%) are using some kind of point system. Most of those who do use points have some method which rewards effort by giving points and takes away points as a penalty. However, the point system is not used any more frequently by successful than less successful directors. Perhaps successful directors have discovered a method of awards which are more likely to stimulate students. Unfortunately, for that hypothesis, it does not matter whether the "payoff" is in trophies or grades. There is no difference in the awards used by different directors.

A series of questions asking how each director solves intonation problems proved equally irrelevant: 13% of the directors attempt to solve intonation problems by buying instruments made by the same company; 14% buy the same mouthpiece; 56% use electronic devices; 28% adjust each instrument; while 78% rely on each student to listen, tune, and adjust his embouchure to secure proper intonation. However, there were no marked differences in the techniques used by nominated and non-nominated directors.

Except for the finding that more students in outstanding bands take lessons from private teachers, the whole series of inquiries about techniques and methods proved rather irrelevant. Some directors use one system and some another. Which system they use is a matter of personal choice. *Techniques and methods are not related in any systematic way to producing an outstanding band.*

The Director's Educational Philosophy

I had hypothesized that there might be some relationship between a director's educational philosophy and his success as a band director. It was hard to predict, in advance, whether a warm director would be more effective than a director who maintained social distance, although I had supposed that a director who involved his students in democratic decision-making and expected them to assume responsibility might be more successful than one who did not. The data came through quite clearly and identified these two types of directors. One type of director is concerned with the total education of his students, fosters warm friendly relations, and involves students in democratic decision-making. The other type of director prefers more social distance, is more authoritarian, does not involve students in decision-making, and has less concern with the student's total educational experience outside of band. Such a fundamental difference in educational philosophy and approach apparently makes no difference and is irrelevant to success.

Significant and Insignificant Relationships

In the above paragraphs we have described a profile of the band director. In most cases, the researcher reports only the statistically significant relationships and tends to ignore the insignificant ones. However, we found that in this instance, the insignificant relationships are just as illuminating as the significant ones. It is just as informative to know what does *not* count in being nominated by a university judge, as to know what does count.

A director's educational background is not important in determining his success nor are the particular methods and techniques he may use in organizing and directing his band. Likewise, his educational philosophy in dealing with students appears unimportant. Directors with varying philosophies are equally successful.

The characteristics which *are* relevant to being nominated for having a successful band will be explored in detail below.

What the "Successful" Director Does

In every field of endeavor there are those men and women who have sufficiently mastered the skills of their profession to rise above the ordinary; so it is in the field of instrumental music. It has been the purpose of this study to identify the major components of "success" used by the high school band directors nominated as outstanding by the university and college directors of their state. These components have been identified based on the data gathered from 222 directors and processed through a computer.

The "Successful" Director Participates in Contests

In earlier chapters we discovered that the successful director is a competing director. Statistical evidence (see Appendix) from this study indicates that preparing soloists and ensembles for contest is significantly related to the number of contests won by the concert band. Those directors who did not enter soloists and ensembles in competitive events were less likely to be nominated by the university directors for having outstanding departments. Undoubtedly, students who prepare solos and work in small ensembles are receiving more intensive tutoring on their instruments than students who do not. It seems reasonable to assume that a director who prepares many soloists and ensembles for contests will have more polished performers for his large groups.

The "Successful" Director Judges Contests

In most states, judges at music contests are likely to be other successful high school and college band directors. If a director can produce a band which is rated high by other band directors who are serving as judges in their state, then he may be asked to serve as a judge in later contests. Data from this study, processed through the computer, statistically supports evidence that successful directors judge more solo, ensemble, and large group contests than do their less successful colleagues. Those who win, judge.

What the "Successful" Director Is

The Successful Director Is An "Organization" Man

As the profile of the successful director emerges from the data, it becomes quite clear that he is an organization man. He actively engages in state and national professional music education organizations and he attends the clinics and workshops sponsored by these organizations.

At clinics the director hears new music, learns about the most recent developments in the field of instrumental music, and meets the other directors who will be judging his groups. He becomes aware of their values and expectations. He learns what kind of music they rate as "good" music, what is considered superior tone quality and intonation, and the kind of dynamic variations they consider good dynamics. He internalizes their norms and goes home better able to create a band to which they will give first division ratings and which they will nominate as outstanding. It is the director who is most fully committed to his profession and its organizational structure who is successful.

The Successful Director Is Confident

You will recall in Chapter 1, that one section of the interview asked each director to complete a "semantic differential" scale on himself and his students. These scales presented bipolar adjectives for various characteristics at the opposite end of a five-inch line. For example, one set of adjectives was bright-dull. The respondent was asked to place a mark on the line separating these two words closest to the adjective that best describes himself or his students, as the case may be. Scores from one through seven are given for various locations on each line (Appendix C).

Psychologists have found this type of personality rating to be a sensitive measure when used to reveal a person's feelings about himself and about others. Because there are no right or wrong answers, the respondent finds it difficult to falsify the ratings. Thus, responses tend to be more spontaneous and less biased than on many other types of personality measures.

In comparing the nominated director's responses with those of his matched colleague, we found statistical evidence which indicates the successful director who sees his students as powerful, demanding, and strong-willed is more successful than one who sees them as powerless and submissive. He believes his students have the power to achieve and they do. His attitude generates a "self-fulfilling prophecy" in which his students tend to perform at the level of his expectation for them.

The "successful" director sees his students as fast and active rather than calm and languid. He assumes that his students are energetic, ready to work, and willing to meet the challenge of a demanding performance. He also has a high opinion of their intelligence. He thinks they are bright and quick, thus feeding back a positive image. Finally, he likes his students. He finds them to be helping, warm, easy to discipline, and sociable rather than difficult and disobedient.

The "successful" director also has significantly more positive feelings about himself that does the less "successful" director. He rates himself as powerful and active, demanding and energetic, rather than weak, powerless, and passive. However, "successful" directors do not rate themselves as more intelligent, more sociable, or better than their less "successful" counterparts rate themselves.

The computer speaks to us through the language of numbers and those readers interested in the statistics which prompted the above observations are referred to index of this book.

Summary

What are the characteristics of the "successful" band director? After analyzing the responses of the band directors in my national sample, the profile of today's "successful" director can be clearly etched. He is a man dedicated to producing quality performing groups, who enters large numbers of students in contests, judges contests himself, goes to clinics and workshops, and works hard in professional organizations. He is committed to public school music and works diligently at meeting the competitive and performance demands of that system. As a person, he sees himself and his students as powerful and energetic — actively mastering challenges. In addition, he regards his students as intelligent, good, and sociable human beings.

Conversely, the less "successful" director is not so dedicated to competitive activities. He does not enter large numbers of students in solo and ensemble contests and is not greatly involved in the professional activities of music education. He has not joined the ranks of those who hold offices and judge contests. He feels that he and his students are less in control of events and are more passive and powerless. He also has a poorer opinion of the intelligence of his students and finds them more disobedient, more difficult to discipline, and less likeable.

Perhaps the most remarkable facet of these profiles is the fact that they have nothing to do with the quality of training the director has received nor his educational philosophy nor his teaching techniques. "Success" depends on the kind of person he is and *his personal commitment and involvement in band activities*. These do not exactly comprise standard courses in the college curricula which prepare men to be band directors and teachers of public school instrumental music.

Chapter IX

Are We Facing a Dilemma
In Instrumental Music?

Most band directors whom I interviewed feel relatively secure in their present situations and believe that their communities are supporting them. Fifty-one per cent of the directors interviewed believe their community regards the marching band as the most important offering of the instrumental department and only five per cent believe their community regards marching band as a "frill" which could be dropped if necessary to cut school costs. Over 59% of the schools have booster clubs which are contributing sizable sums of money to support the instrumental program. Eighty-three per cent of the directors believe the school board would be willing to finance additional equipment; 84% believe their principals would be willing to approve the expense of extra transportation for a special program; 78% report that the city council would put up city flags for a band event if it were asked; 75% report that the mayor would be willing to make a public statement supporting the band; and 86% say that local merchants are willing to donate money to band activities. The typical band director believes his school board, school administration, and community are solidly behind him. Band is not regarded as an academic subject and students do not receive full credit for band toward graduation but directors are certain that band is not regarded as an expendable "frill."

Although the school and community appear to be satisfied with our present educational role which emphasizes performance, certain voices of concern have arisen among educators themselves. The following quotations are from men who feel the need for developing a broader musical base. From a supervisor of music of a major California City:

Personally, I am disturbed by the fact that only 15% of the secondary students (grades 9-12) are ever brought into contact with a formal music experience of some type. New thinking is going to be necessary to develop music programs that can be offered to *all* secondary students as part of a total education program that must include art and music. To me, it is pitiful to see so many gifted students who are so knowledgeable in math, science, foreign languages, and are practially illiterate in the areas of fine arts.

If we believe music can stand on the same footing as English or social studies, then we must be prepared to teach all children, as these departments do . . . If music is to fulfill its role as a fundamental part of the curriculum, then our offer-

ing must be designed for all students, not just a few.
— Angelo Giaudrone, CMEA News (April-May, 19   p. 16)
    The young musicians of today, according to composers and conductors, are generally very well-trained in the techniques of playing their instruments — better trained, in fact, than were the young musicians of previous generations. But despite their superior technique, these musicians are too often poorly equipped in knowledge, understanding, and experience of a professional nature. They can play the notes, but they cannot play the music.
    Music education in the high schools of the United States involves less than 20% of the students. Most of these students are engaged in choral or instrumental performance which generally provides only limited opportunity for a systematic study of music as an art. — Judith Murphy and George Sullivan, *Music in American Society: An Interpretive Report of the Tanglewood Symposium*, Music Educators National Conference, 1968, p. 47.

These voices of concern are echoed in this study as well as in my own experiences. Several provocative questions persist.

It There a Conflict Between Educational and Performance Goals?

What happens to education values when polished musical performance is the primary standard for judging the quality of a band, orchestra, or chorus? Two personal experiences will serve to illustrate the kind of impasse presented by these opposing sets of values.

While adjudicating a district music contest, I heard the concert band from an affluent community with a well-known and highly regarded music department. Although the school enrolled over 3,200 students and the instrumental program of the high school included over 250 students, the concert band which appeared at the music contest consisted of 45 carefully auditioned and rigorously screened young musicians. Only a few spectators and parents sat in a nearly empty auditorium. The band's performance was so technically brilliant and exciting, I temporarily forgot my role as judge and became totally engrossed in their sparkling presentation. The performance of this high school band was among the most thrilling I have ever heard and represented the ultimate product of public school music in America.

The next band on the schedule crowded the stage with students wearing old, out-of-style uniforms but which were clean and recently pressed. The auditorium rapidly filled with parents and there was a feeling of tension and excitement among the students and the spectators. The performance was a memorable as that of the preceding band, but for different reasons. Although the band played compositions performed several times during the day by other bands, the music was rather difficult to recognize. As an adjudicator schooled in the tradition of musical excellence, I saw a large group of technically immature students with little conception of intonation or the rudiments of quality music. By any musical standards this was a very poor group. Yet, as a music educator, I saw a different picture. I knew these students were from a small, financially handicapped high school whose administration had experienced difficulty in securing a band director. Their new, young director had involved almost 25% of the students in his school in the band and had apparently brought them all to perform at the music festival. Although they were of high school age, most were beginners as music performers. They had been recruited from the high school student body. On any measure of student interest, student progress, student participation, and community support, this band would rate very high. But it was not being evaluated on these characteristics. By the criterion of musical excellence, this band was a disaster. It received the lowest rating.

The predicament of education vs. performance values again presented itself while I was interviewing in Texas. A small high school in the valley near the Mexican border appeared, by chance, as a matched school in my sample. Driving down the rural highway, I almost missed the town because it consists of only one restaurant, a grocery store, and a bar. The school building is over 60 years old and the high school has just over 400 students. Most of the families of the children attending this school are migrant workers who earn less than $2,000 per year. Their children leave school early in the spring to follow the crops with their families and return late in the fall. The school has an educational program designed for the children of migrant workers and a band program that includes 72 students — 18% of the student body. The Mexican-American director is 35 years old, has been teaching in this same school for 14 years, and earns a salary of $5,600. He seeks supplementary employment during the summer in order to support his family. The year I visited him, he had entered 33 students (46% of his band) in the state solo contest. He holds five sectional rehearsals per week after school. Each year he takes his band to the state music contest and competes, unsuccessfully, with bands from more stable and affluent communities. His students return home discouraged and disappointed. I found the director frustrated and humiliated. There was no way for him to "succeed" in a performance-oriented system except by abandoning his little school and seeking a position in a more privileged community. This he refused to do. Yet, by any standard of educational values, his achievements are exemplary.

Those directors who choose to work with disadvantaged students and assume the most demanding educational roles in our society are penalized in a performance-oriented system. If they were judged by the educational distance they have come with their students rather than by the musical standard achieved, many of them would be rated far higher than the director with the band from the wealthy neighborhood who brings only his outstanding 45 players to the contest. Must educational values and performance values conflict? Can this impasse be resolved?

Is Competition a Yardstick for Excellence?

This study has shown that, in general, the competitive aspects of music are not perpetuated by school administrators, although parents and students give more support to bands which win contests. Competition is mainly sustained by the internal structure of our own professional social system. Those directors who succeed in this system, that is, win many competitive honors and, perhaps, move into college positions, are those who have produced outstanding performing groups. Those who "succeed" in this fashion join the select group of directors who judge the performing groups of their fellow band directors at marching and concert band contests. Thus, the value system is perpetuated which rewards those directors who have produced polished performing groups. Special difficulties which a director may have because of the social status or background of his students are not taken into account. There is primarily a single yardstick — *performance*.

Is the Score the Curriculum?

The original questionnaire asked each director to describe his course of study and curriculum for band. I dropped the question after the first 50 interviews because the responses were almost identical. In each case, the director interpreted the question to mean, "What rehearsal techniques do you use?" and proceeded to give me a detailed account of the procedures he uses to warm up and tune his band.

If I had asked a teacher of mathematics or social studies or science to describe the curriculum of his department, there would have been no confusion. He would have outlined the subject matter covered in the course of one year, the kinds of skills and information a student is expected to acquire, and possibly listed the books, films, field trips, experiments, and projects which he uses to accomplish his educational goals.

As band directors we have been preoccupied with preparing our next performance and have taken little time to develop a coherent music curriculum. There are few carefully planned courses of study designed to teach students the fundamentals of music theory, introduce them systematically to the great composers, or assist them in comprehending the fascinating metamorphosis of musical form and style through the broad sweep of man's history. Instead, our students concentrate on acquiring the technical competence necessary to play the scores which we decide will make an interesting program for our next audience or will please our colleagues who will be judging the next contest.

Is There An Evaluation Vacuum

How do band directors decide what grade a student should receive? Look closely at figure 7. You will note that almost every director uses some subjective evaluation of "responsibility" and "cooperation" as the cornerstone of his system to evaluate his marching band. A majority also take attendance into account and above half consider "marching ability." Only 41% give the student a performance test on his instrument to ascertain how well he has mastered the music. A negligible 7% rely on written tests for grading. What the student contributes to the group by taking a responsible attitude and being cooperative is more important to the director than what the student himself learns from his experience because it is the group which will perform as a collectivity. Thus those behavior factors which preserve the band as a performing organization — responsibility, cooperation, and attendance — are rewarded more frequently than the acquisition of individual music knowledge and skills. The majority of band directors do not take the latter into account at all in grading for marching band.

Attendance is easy to record and evaluate but "responsibility" and "cooperation" are ambiguous characteristics which can be assessed only subjectively. Eleven per cent of the directors reported that they had "no grading formula," an additional 2% let each student grade himself, and 7% let everyone start with an "A" and work down. Another 3% did not have to face the dilemma because their schools do not require grades for band — just credit or no credit.

The pattern of weighing responsibility and cooperation most heavily in grading for band is nationwide. Attendance is mentioned as a factor in grading by twice as many Pacific Coast directors as Midwestern directors while other regions fall between the two extremes. Southern directors are much more likely than directors in other regions to give each student a playing test on his instrument and to use that as part of the evaluation. However, the uniformities in evaluation from region to region are much more conspicuous than these minor differences.

In concert season the pressure for performance continues but the direction of effort shifts and the grading system used by band directors reflects the change. There is more emphasis on instrumental technique; 67% of the directors report giving tests in which students are graded on their instrumental performance. The number of directors using written tests increases from 7% to 29% and the percentage using a point system declines slightly. Two new evaluation methods appear — grading students on special reports and other assignments (26%) and grading students according to the chair they occupy in their section (22%). Although the emphasis is slightly different, the focus is still on performance and contribution to the group.

However, the best evidence of the vacuum in the evaluation system is the number of "F's" and the number of "A's" which were given by each director in grading period just prior to the interview. Seventy-eight per cent of the directors gave no "f's," and only 9% of the directors gave three or more "F's." Clearly, almost nobody fails band. On the other hand, directors, on the average, gave 49 "A's" in concert band. Since the typical high school concert band has 81 members, this means that approximately 60% of the students in the high school bands in this sample received a grade of "A."

Why so few "F's" and so many "A's?" The answer lies in at least two directions. First, if grades are based mainly on attendance, responsibility, and cooperation, then many students can easily meet these expectations and, consequently, will receive an "A."

Second, and perhaps more important, the band director, unlike most teachers, is in a vulnerable position vis-a-vis his students. He is expected to produce polished performing groups. To do this, he needs to keep his bandsmen enrolled in band so that he will have a full instrumentation. He depends heavily on the maturity of his juniors and seniors and the loss of even one or two key students can significantly impair his organization. The performance orientation of his field has left him without adequate resources for replacing any student losses. only 10.6% of the high schools studied have a program for beginners. Therefore, he hesitates to alienate students by giving them low grades because he needs them.

Incidentally, after looking at these figures and writing this section, I went to school to locate my own grade book from last spring. You guessed it: 114 "A's, 32 "B's," 4 "C's," 0 "D's," and 2 "F's."

Summary

Although the school and community appear to be satisfied with instrumental music in the public schools, voices of concern are being raised among educators themselves. They are chiefly concerned because only a relatively small number of secondary students are being brought into contact with a formal music experience.

These voices of concern are echoed in this study and call attention to provocative questions which ask:

Is there a conflict between educational and performance goals?

Is competition a yardstick for excellence?

Is the score being played the only curriculum?

Is there an evaluation vacuum?

Tradition in American schools has emphasized training the performing musician with relatively little emphasis on training the listener.

However, it is not fair to condemn performances *per se* because some directors or schools multiply an excessive number of performances. Music is created to be performed and bands, orchestras, and choirs are organized with the express purpose of re-creating musical compositions. Someplace between multiple performances and the "purpose" of our performing groups, must arise a philosophical question . . . *"Is performance total music education?"*

Conclusion

This study, based on 222 interviews widely scattered over 17,500 miles, identifies those characteristics which comprise a "successful" high school band and band director in the United States.

The 65,000 responses were analyzed by computer and only those variables which proved to be statistically significant were recorded.

Although this study is primarily focused on the band director, choir, orchestral, as well as future public school educators will discover several common denominators running through these data. For example, student motivation, promoting, finances, and competition are common to *all* directors. What is basically required of the "successful" director remains the same whether he is leading a band, orchestra, or choir. The profile of the "successful" director is sculptured in bold figures by the computer.

In the Appendix is an impressive matrix of intercorrelations for those educators who are statistically inclined. Here are listed certain professional activities in which the director engages and the reader may examine the weight of each variable as it is related to the profile of success. (Appendix B).

In the Coda which follows are some personal conclusions I have drawn from this study. These are presented primarily to stimulate additional thinking which may lead to the solving of some pressing problems being faced by public school music.

Coda

While writing Chapter 8 describing the profile of the "successful" American high school band director, I was amazed by the similarity of the computer's description of the typical director and my own experience. I was a trumpet player in my high school band and decided to become an instrumental teacher because of the influence of my high school band director. My college training concentrated entirely on preparation for public school music and I completed my Master's Degree at Northwestern University. During my first year of teaching in a high school with a student body of 150, I was asked to teach civics and to direct the choir as well as the band. Since then, I have taught only instrumental music.

The decision to travel 17,500 miles and visit 222 directors was motivated by a desire to know what my colleagues were doing in their various departments scattered throughout the United States. However, as I talked with them, they seemed surprised by the simplicity of this motivation and many wondered why I did not turn this experience into an advanced degree. The profile of the typical director described in Chapter 8 is my best answer. "What would I like to be doing 5 years from now?" Of course, the same thing I am doing today — directing a band!

However, even though the book is finished, the score is not complete. Like some melodies, the theme of this book keeps running through my mind. Performing groups are an essential part of American public schools and most directors in this study feel that their school and community support the role that performing groups are now playing in the educational development of their young people.

Under the magnifying qualities of 222 interviews, certain weaknesses also become apparent. In this final Coda I will try to pinpoint areas which appear to need attention if music education is to continue to grow and expand.

Two major goals in music education are (1) to teach students to comprehend intellectually and to enjoy emotionally their musical heritage as listeners, and (2) to prepare students as instrumentalists and vocalists so they can produce music. Historically, public school music (instrumental and vocal) has emphasized the latter and, for all practical purposes, ignored the former. This is unfortunate because public school music is a caricature of what it could be if these two aspects had been kept in balance from the beginning. It staggers the imagination to contemplate the immensity of music in American schools if educators would begin a concentrated effort to include the 80% of our students in high school who are not presently engaged in some form of music activity.

But equally important as the neglected 80% are the 20% who *are* now receiving a highly specialized diet of performance. These young people spend five hours a week during three to four years of their high school lives in a performing group, more time than they spend in any other single school subject. Yet they frequently emerge from this experience as musical technicians rather than musically educated adults.

Why Haven't We Seen the Picture Before?

Most instrumental and vocal teachers in public schools have never really analyzed what is happening because they are already working to the limit of their energies doing the same things all of us are doing — giving performances, raising money, or recruiting promising beginners.

Since American public schools have never provided a comprehensive music education for *all* students, it doesn't occur to the overworked band director, orchestra director, or vocal teacher to wonder about the other 80% of the student body.

A second reason we have not seen the total picture is that the values of the performance ethic are deeply ingrained in our concept of who we are professionally and what we are doing as band directors. Each of us has come to measure our worth as a music educator in terms of the number of first division ratings and contests won. The pervasiveness of this value system is illustrated by a simple assumption made, unconsciously, at the beginning of this study. In the letters mailed to the university directors, I told them I wanted to study "successful" band departments and asked them to select the 20 "best" bands in their state. No further instruction was given. Yet, directors from 13 states who did not know each other or know me understood exactly what was intended. We share the same value system. A "successful" band means an outstanding performing group!

A third reason that we have not fully seen the picture is because the performance ethic has been institutionalized and therefore accepted without question. Beginning in the early 1900's, an elaborate social structure developed in every state in the United States to direct and monitor music competitions. Each state has some mechanism for selecting and training judges; has developed standardized forms and procedures for assessing music performances; has developed a system for ranking schools by size so that only schools of approximately the same size will be competing against each other; has organized a staff of persons who schedule contests and keep records of the results.

A value system embodied in a social structure is almost impervious to change. Man's social institutions are among the more enduring of his creations. Through them the performance ethic is conveyed to each new generation of music teachers who, in turn, measure their worth by the quality of their performing groups and do whatever is necessary to fulfill the values they have been taught. The uniformity in educational background and experience of the band directors found in this survey testifies to this fact.

A fourth reason we have not seen the total picture, is closely related to the institutionalization of the competitive motive in music education in America. Probably the single most significant finding of this study was the integral relationship between "success" as defined by university judges and participation in the institutional structure of competitive music performance. Those who are regarded as a "success" not only enter their concert bands in competition but also prepare many soloists and ensembles. They serve as judges at large and small group contests, take their turn playing host to contests, belong to the professional organizations of music educators, and hold offices in those organizations.

It is a characteristic of all social systems that they reward those who best fulfill the expectations of the system by giving them positions of leadership in the system. Such symbolic rewards are frequently more important in human motivation than more tangible rewards. As a result, institutionalized competitive music is a self-perpetuating system because each new generation of leaders is chosen by those who have gone before. In this fashion, the values of the performance ethic are maintained. Only those who have shown by their behavior that they not only believe that developing performers of music is the most important task of music education but are capable of producing competent performers are chosen as leaders.

The final reason we have not seen the total picture is because our emphasis on performance is encouraged and supported by persons outside the field of music. We cannot ignore the fact that community support and student support were positively correlated with the number of first division ratings won by the concert band. Communities enjoy the flash and excitement of the halftime show and the competitive spirit of the contest. They like to back a "winning" band just as they like to back a winning football team. Public school music has justified its existence for half a century on this basis and is now partially propelled by the momentum of that justification and the community expectations it has fostered. Instrumental music has succeeded so well in providing entertainment for athletic events and other social activities, it would be difficult to extricate it from the consequences of its own splendid showmanship.

Today, music education faces an uncertain future. The public schools have never given students a comprehensive music education. Music teachers have never insisted that cultivating appreciation for our musical heritage is important for *every* student and that music understanding and music appreciation belong in the curriculum just as surely as history or literature.

Band directors, orchestra directors, and vocal teachers are not trained for the task of comprehensive music education. We have been trained to be directors, technicians, and performers. We are ill-prepared to develop a music curriculum which would go beyond the scores for the next performance and include units on music theory, form and analysis, music history, or music appreciation. Yet, this is our challenge, this is the wave of the future. Where will we go from here?

APPENDIX

1. Letter to University Judges

Hello,

I am presently taking a sabbatical to study many of the successful band departments in the nation. Next month I will be traveling to your state to interview twenty band directors. I would like to discuss with them the organizational structure of their departments and later report my findings in a series of magazine articles and in book form.

In order to give a fair evaluation of the work being done in your state, it is quite imperative to select twenty of your **best** bands.

Would you be kind enough to look over the two lists which are attached to this letter and nominate ten large schools and ten small schools that you would like to see represent your state in this sample. Please list them in rank order and return the list to me in the self-addressed envelope which is enclosed.

Sincerely yours,
R. Jack Mercer
Chairman of Band Affairs
Ontario, California

2. YOUR BAND'S PERSONALITY

Directions:

Will you now think about your band as if it has a personality. Below are listed characteristics we would like to examine. Place an "X" toward the side of the scale that best describes your band. Check every item, but never put more than one "X" on any scale.

Demanding								Not demanding
Passive								Active
Intelligent								Unintelligent
Not helping								Helping
Warm								Cold
Powerful								Powerless
Lethargic								Fast
Bright								Dull
Difficult Discipline								Easy Discipline
Sociable								Unsociable
Weak Willed								Strong Willed
Energetic								Languid
Slow								Quick
Obedient								Disobedient
Hard								Soft
Assertive								Submissive
Calm								Excitable
Accelerated								Retarded
Bad								Good
Extroverted								Introverted

3. YOUR OWN PERSONALITY

Directions:

Will you now think about your own personality. Using the same scale that was used to examine the band, indicate how you yourself would appear on this scale.

Demanding							Not demanding
Passive							Active
Intelligent							Unintelligent
Not helping							Helping
Warm							Cold
Powerful							Powerless
Lethargic							Fast
Bright							Dull
Difficult Discipline							Easy Discipline
Sociable							Unsociable
Weak Willed							Strong Willed
Energetic							Languid
Slow							Quick
Obedient							Disobedient
Hard							Soft
Assertive							Submissive
Calm							Excitable
Accelerated							Retarded
Bad							Good
Extroverted							Introverted

These attitudinal scales were selected items from the semantic differential scales developed by Osgood.[1] Instructions for completing the ratings are very simple. Each director received a sheet of paper on which there were 20 pairs of adjectives. (A copy of the rating form is in the Appendix.) Each pair consisted of adjectives describing the two extremes of 20 characteristics, i.e. active – passive; bright – dull; helping – not helping; powerful – powerless, etc. The adjectives in each pair were separated by a five-inch line divided into seven equal segments. The director was asked to place an "X" on each of the lines at the point where he believed most of his students belong. When he finished rating his students on each of the 20 dichotomies, he was given a second sheet of paper containing the same 20 adjective pairs and was asked to rate himself on each of these characteristics.

Each rating was scored from one to seven depending on the segment of the line on which the "X" was located. Pairs of adjectives were selected so they would measure five personality traits: power, activity, intelligence, goodness, and sociability. Ratings on four related pairs of adjectives were added together to get the total score on each personality trait. Scores could range from 4 through 28.[2]

[1] Charles Osgood and J.G. Snider, *Semantic Differential*, Chicago: Aldine Press, 1969.

[2]

PERSONALITY TRAIT	ADJECTIVE PAIR SCORES ADDED TO GET SCORE ON PERSONALITY TRAIT

POWER — demanding-not demanding; powerful-powerless; strong willed-weak willed; assertive-submissive

ACTIVITY — active-passive; fast-lethargic; energetic-languid; excitable-calm

INTELLIGENCE — intelligent-unintelligent; bright-dull; quick-slow; accelerated-retarded

GOODNESS — helping-not helping; easy to discipline-hard to discipline; obedient-disobedient; good-bad

SOCIABILITY — warm-cold; sociable-unsociable; soft-hard; extroverted-introverted

What the Successful Director Does [a]

	Success Variables			Judges Contests		Contests Participants		Organizational Man				
— PROFESSIONAL VARIABLES —	Average university rank score	# Concert contests won	# Marching contests won	# Solo & ensemble contests judged	# Large group contests judged	# Students entering solo contests	# Ensembles entered in contests	# Clinic & workshops attended	# State music organ. joined	# National music organ. joined	# offices held	# Contests hosted
Average University rank	X	.27	—	.27	.26	.18	.16	.19	—	.27	—	—
# Concert Contests won	.27	X	.20	.23	.35	.23	.33	.21	—	—	.18	—
# Marching Contests won	—	.20	X	—	—	—	—	—	.15	—	—	—
PROFESSIONAL ACTIVITIES												
# Solo & Ensemble contests judged	.27	.23	—	X	.48	.38	.34	.20	—	.29	.33	.15
# Large group contests judged	.26	.35	—	.48	X	.31	.24	—	—	.20	.23	—
# Students entering solo contests	.18	.23	—	.38	.31	X	.54	.17	.15	.16	.17	.27
# Ensembles entered in contests	.16	.33	—	.34	.24	.54	X	(.14)	.15	.20	.17	.15
# Clinics & workshops attended	.19	.21	—	.20	—	.17	(.14)	X	.28	—	.22	—
# State music organizations joined	—	—	.15	—	—	.15	.15	.28	X	.32	(.14)	—
# National music organizations joined	.27	—	—	.29	.20	.16	.20	.22	.32	X	.24	—
# Offices held	—	.18	—	.33	.23	.17	.17	.22	(.14)	.24	X	.17
# Contests hosted	—	—	—	.15	—	.27	.15	—	—	—	.17	X

[a] Any correlation of .15 or higher is significant at the .05 level; any correlation of .21 or higher is significant at the .01 level.

3. MATRIX OF INTERCORRELATIONS

As we examine the matrix entitled "What the Successful Director Does," you will notice a boxed-in area entitled Success Variables. Under this title are listed three sub-headings:

1. Average University Rank Score
2. Number of Concert Contests Won
3. Number of Marching Contests Won

You will recall that our study is built around those departments recommended by university judges and this has become our primary "success" variable. On the basis of these nominations, each director received an average university rank score. During the interview, each director also reported the number of marching contests his band had won and the number of first division ratings he had received in the most recent contest series. These ratings were used as two additional measures of "success."

The matrix is designed to compare all the activities listed below the boxed area with these three measures of success, i.e. Average University Rank Score; Number of Concert Contests Won; and Number of Marching Contests Won.

The matrix can be read either down the columns or across depending on what activities are to be compared. For example, if a comparison is desired between the "Success" variables themselves, it can be found by reading both directions.

Look now at the matrix itself. Notice the .27 located **under** Average University Rank Score, and **beside** No. Concert Contests Won. This indicates that University judges are more likely to nominate bands which have high concert band contest ratings. Now note that **under** Average University Rank Score and **beside** No. Marching Contests Won, there is no score. This means that university judges **do not** take marching band performance into account when they nominate outstanding bands. The basic values of the evaluation system are evident in this simple set of correlations. Concert band performance is important but marching band performance is irrelevant to "success" in the eyes of the university judge.

There are many directors with outstanding concert bands who also have good marching bands. Hence, there is a correlation of .20 between marching contests won and the number of first division concert ratings. However, the marching contests are incidental rather than central to being nominated. In other words, a director who **only** has a good marching band is not likely to be nominated. A director with an outstanding concert band is likely to be nominated. He may also have a good marching band, but that is not important in his being nominated.

4. THE INSIGNIFICANT POSITION OF MARCHING
BAND IN THE "SUCCESS" COMPLEX

The inconsequential position of marching band in the "Success Complex" is further reinforced when we **read down** the column for each of the "success" variables. For example, the "success" variable called **Average University Rank Score** is related to six of the professional activities in which directors engage:

.27 — Number of solo and ensemble contests judged
.26 — Large group contests judged
.18 — Number of students entering solo contests
.16 — Number of ensembles entered in contests
.19 — Number of clinics and workshops attended
.27 — Number of national music organizations joined

Turning now to the "success" variable called **Number of Concert Contests Won** and reading **down,** we find it is also related to six of the professional activities in which directors participate.

.23 — Number of solo and ensemble contests judged
.35 — Large group contests judged
.23 — Number of students entering solo contests
.33 — Number of ensembles entered in contests
.21 — Number of clinics and workshops attended
.18 — Number of offices held

Now as we compare the "success" variable called **Number of Marching Contests Won,** we find it is related to one professional activity:

.15 — Number of State Music organizations joined

This puts **Marching Band Contests Won** in a weak position because it is correlated with only one other professional activity and that one is not correlated with either of the other measures of "success." Thus, statistical evidence indicates that a director does not have to have a winning marching band to be highly regarded by university judges but his concert band is of critical importance.

Professional Activity Variables

Looking again at the matrix, you will note three major areas listed to the right of the "Success" variables. The first is called **Judges Contest** and has two sub-headings:

1. Number of Solo & Ensemble Contests Judged
2. Number of Large Group Contests Judged

The second is called **Participants in Contests** and also has two sub-headings:

1. Number of Students Entering Solo Contests
2. Number of Ensembles Entered in Contests

The third major area is entitled **Organizational Man** and it is divided into five sub-headings:

1. Number of Clinics & Workshops Attended
2. Number of State Music Organizations Joined
3. Number of National Music Organizations Joined
4. Number of Offices Held
5. Number of Contests Hosted

You will note that these sub-headings listed under Professional **Variables** are listed again to the left side of the matrix as Professional **Activities**. Through a mathematical formula called correlational analysis these items are evaluated to determine their importance in the formula of "success." If there is any relation between a "success" variable and a "Professional Activity" variable, it will appear on the matrix as a number beginning with .15. The higher the number is about .15, the more weight it brings to the "success" formula. (You will notice that we have reported some correlations that were almost, but not significant. They are indicated by parentheses, e.g. (.14)).

5. CORRELATIONS BETWEEN PERSONALITY RATINGS AND MEASURES OF SUCCESS

WHAT THE SUCCESSFUL DIRECTOR IS [a]

Correlations Between Personality Ratings
and Measures of Success

The Director Interprets	Average University Rank	Number Concert Contests Won

AS THE "SUCCESSFUL" DIRECTOR SEES HIS STUDENTS:

	Average University Rank	Number Concert Contests Won
Powerful	.28	.15
Active	.29	.22
Intelligent	.21	.16
Good	.24	.19
Sociable	.19	-

AS THE "SUCCESSFUL" DIRECTOR SEES HIMSELF:

	Average University Rank	Number Concert Contests Won
Powerful	.23	.18
Active	.21	.18
Intelligent	-	-
Good	-	-
Sociable	-	-

This correlation compares the student and director's personality ratings with the two measures of "success," i.e. the average university rank given by university judges and the number of concert contests won. Only the "successful" director's personality rating appears on this matrix because the correlation was set up to compare the nominated director with the matched director.

You will note a consistent pattern of positive correlations between personality ratings given by the directors and the other two "success" variables — average university rank, and the number of concert contests won. Keep in mind that .15 is

[a] Any linear correlation of .15 or above is significant at the .05 level; any correlation of .21 or above is significant at the .01 level.

the beginning of significance in these correlations and weight of significance increases with every number added.

It is immediately apparent to the reader that there is a close relationship between how the director sees his students and the average university rank. Reading down we see:

.28 — powerful
.29 — active
.21 — intelligent
.24 — good
.19 — sociable

The same is true when comparing the attitude of the director toward his students and the Number of Concert Contests Won:

.15 — powerful
.22 — active
.16 — intelligent
.19 — good

Thus we can statistically claim that "successful" directors have significantly more positive attitudes toward their students in every area studied.

DATE DUE

4-7-77			

HIGHSMITH 45-220